Mandatory Minimum Sentencing

Other Books of Related Interest:

Opposing Viewpoints Series

American Values

Crime and Criminals

Criminal Justice

Domestic Violence

Racial Profiling

Sexual Violence

At Issue Series

Guns and Crime

Is Torture Ever Justified?

Racial Profiling

Current Controversies Series

Family Violence

Guns and Violence

Prisons

"Congress shall make no law . . . abridging the freedom of speech, or of the press."

First Amendment to the U.S. Constitution

The basic foundation of our democracy is the First Amendment guarantee of freedom of expression. The Opposing Viewpoints Series is dedicated to the concept of this basic freedom and the idea that it is more important to practice it than to enshrine it.

Mandatory Minimum Sentencing

Margaret Haerens, Book Editor

GREENHAVEN PRESS
A part of Gale, Cengage Learning

Detroit • New York • San Francisco • New Haven, Conn • Waterville, Maine • London

Christine Nasso, *Publisher*
Elizabeth Des Chenes, *Managing Editor*

For more information, contact:
Greenhaven Press
27500 Drake Rd.
Farmington Hills, MI 48331-3535
Or you can visit our Internet site at gale.cengage.com

LIBRARY OF CONGRESS CATALOGING-IN-PUBLICATION DATA

Mandatory minimum sentencing / Margaret Haerens, book editor.
p. cm. -- (Opposing viewpoints)
Includes bibliographical references and index.
ISBN 978-0-7377-4775-1 (hardcover) -- ISBN 978-0-7377-4776-8 (pbk.)
1. Mandatory sentences--United States--Juvenile literature. 2. Sentences (Criminal procedure)--United States--Juvenile literature. I. Haerens, Margaret.
KF9685.M339 2010
345.73'0772--dc22

2009050926

Printed in the United States of America
1 2 3 4 5 6 7 14 13 12 11 10

Contents

Chapter 4: What Are Some Alternatives to Mandatory Minimum Sentencing?

Why Consider Opposing Viewpoints?

> *"The only way in which a human being can make some approach to knowing the whole of a subject is by hearing what can be said about it by persons of every variety of opinion and studying all modes in which it can be looked at by every character of mind. No wise man ever acquired his wisdom in any mode but this."*
>
> *John Stuart Mill*

In our media-intensive culture it is not difficult to find differing opinions. Thousands of newspapers and magazines and dozens of radio and television talk shows resound with differing points of view. The difficulty lies in deciding which opinion to agree with and which "experts" seem the most credible. The more inundated we become with differing opinions and claims, the more essential it is to hone critical reading and thinking skills to evaluate these ideas. Opposing Viewpoints books address this problem directly by presenting stimulating debates that can be used to enhance and teach these skills. The varied opinions contained in each book examine many different aspects of a single issue. While examining these conveniently edited opposing views, readers can develop critical thinking skills such as the ability to compare and contrast authors' credibility, facts, argumentation styles, use of persuasive techniques, and other stylistic tools. In short, the Opposing Viewpoints Series is an ideal way to attain the higher-level thinking and reading skills so essential in a culture of diverse and contradictory opinions.

In addition to providing a tool for critical thinking, Opposing Viewpoints books challenge readers to question their own strongly held opinions and assumptions. Most people form their opinions on the basis of upbringing, peer pressure, and personal, cultural, or professional bias. By reading carefully balanced opposing views, readers must directly confront new ideas as well as the opinions of those with whom they disagree. This is not to argue simplistically that everyone who reads opposing views will—or should—change his or her opinion. Instead, the series enhances readers' understanding of their own views by encouraging confrontation with opposing ideas. Careful examination of others' views can lead to the readers' understanding of the logical inconsistencies in their own opinions, perspective on why they hold an opinion, and the consideration of the possibility that their opinion requires further evaluation.

Evaluating Other Opinions

To ensure that this type of examination occurs, Opposing Viewpoints books present all types of opinions. Prominent spokespeople on different sides of each issue as well as well-known professionals from many disciplines challenge the reader. An additional goal of the series is to provide a forum for other, less known, or even unpopular viewpoints. The opinion of an ordinary person who has had to make the decision to cut off life support from a terminally ill relative, for example, may be just as valuable and provide just as much insight as a medical ethicist's professional opinion. The editors have two additional purposes in including these less known views. One, the editors encourage readers to respect others' opinions—even when not enhanced by professional credibility. It is only by reading or listening to and objectively evaluating others' ideas that one can determine whether they are worthy of consideration. Two, the inclusion of such viewpoints encourages the important critical thinking skill of objectively evaluating an author's credentials and bias. This evaluation will illuminate an author's reasons for taking a particular stance on an issue and will aid in readers' evaluation of the author's ideas.

It is our hope that these books will give readers a deeper understanding of the issues debated and an appreciation of the complexity of even seemingly simple issues when good and honest people disagree. This awareness is particularly important in a democratic society such as ours in which people enter into public debate to determine the common good. Those with whom one disagrees should not be regarded as enemies but rather as people whose views deserve careful examination and may shed light on one's own.

Thomas Jefferson once said that "difference of opinion leads to inquiry, and inquiry to truth." Jefferson, a broadly educated man, argued that "if a nation expects to be ignorant and free . . . it expects what never was and never will be." As individuals and as a nation, it is imperative that we consider the opinions of others and examine them with skill and discernment. The Opposing Viewpoints Series is intended to help readers achieve this goal.

David L. Bender and Bruno Leone,
Founders

Introduction

> *"It's easy to run for office saying, 'I was tough on crime.' No member of Congress has to look at an individual or an individual's family and see the unfairness of that sentence being imposed and the devastating impact that it has on the family."*
>
> *Jack B. Weinstein, federal judge*

In September 2004, a Baltimore man named Derrick Kimbrough was indicted in federal court in Virginia on four drug-related counts: conspiracy to distribute both crack and powder cocaine, possession with intent to distribute more than fifty grams of crack cocaine, possession with intent to distribute powder cocaine, and possession of a firearm in furtherance of a drug trafficking offense. He pled guilty. Under the federal mandatory drug sentencing laws, Kimbrough faced a sentence of between fifteen years and life in prison. The district court, however, reconfigured his sentence to 228 to 270 months in prison, a higher sentence justified by the court because his offense involved both crack and powder cocaine. The district judge noted that if Kimbrough's crime had involved powder cocaine only, his sentencing range would have been 97 to 106 months. He was later sentenced to 180 months in prison because of mandatory minimum sentencing laws. Kimbrough's lawyer appealed the harsh sentence, and eventually the Fourth Circuit Court of Appeals vacated it, arguing that any sentence that fell outside the sentencing guidelines range was unreasonable if that sentence was based on a policy disagreement with the fact that crack cocaine offenses are punished more harshly than powder cocaine offenses. The case then was accepted for review by the U.S. Supreme Court.

Kimbrough was caught in what is known as the crack-powder cocaine disparity. Under federal law, an offender caught with five grams of crack faces the same five-year mandatory minimum prison term as a powder cocaine offender in possession of five hundred grams. These wildly disparate sentencing laws result in a one-hundred-to-one ratio in sentencing. Legislators had originally justified the disparity by arguing that crack cocaine was much more dangerous than powder cocaine and had much more pervasive and insidious effects on American communities. At the time, such thinking was understandable. In 1986, when these new laws were being introduced at the federal level, the crack cocaine epidemic was at its peak and the devastating impact on urban communities was being felt in the form of skyrocketing crack addiction rates and crime rates. At the time, Congress felt a responsibility to act and to act strongly against the scourge that was spreading through so many regions of the country.

However, the crack-powder cocaine disparity almost immediately raised concern and engendered controversy. Federal judges have long been some of the most vocal critics against the one-hundred-to-one ratio. One recurring criticism by the federal judiciary is that the law is simply unjust: it punishes nonviolent street-corner crack peddlers more harshly than major powder cocaine traffickers. Moreover, they underscore the unfairness of putting a first-time offender in jail for five years for a thimble-size amount of crack, thereby splitting up families and causing undue hardship when there are viable alternatives, such as drug courts. Another criticism of federal crack cocaine mandatory sentences as they stand is that the disproportionate penalties treat African Americans unfairly. The statistics show that African Americans account for 80 to 90 percent of defendants convicted of crack offenses, and whites and Hispanics for more than 70 percent of powder offenders. These numbers, experts believe, illuminate the disproportionate effects of the federally mandated crack cocaine sentencing laws on certain communities, an unintentional effect that they argue must be taken into account and rectified by correcting the crack-powder cocaine disparity.

In fact, reforming the crack-powder disparity is a movement gaining ground in the Congress and the court system. In 2005 the U.S. Supreme Court came out with a benchmark ruling on sentencing, *United States v. Booker*. In this case, the Court found that mandatory sentencing guidelines violate a defendant's constitutional rights and made the federal sentencing guidelines "advisory." In late 2007 the U.S. Supreme Court ruled, in *United States v. Kimbrough*, that judges have the authority to sentence individuals below the recommended federal sentencing guideline recommendation in crack cocaine cases. That same year the U.S. Sentencing Commission (USSC) offered an amendment to lower guideline sentencing recommendations by two levels, saving defendants approximately sixteen months of prison time. Then, the USSC made the amendment retroactive, saving offenders an average of 27 months on their prison terms. Congress is also working on several bills that will directly address the crack-powder cocaine disparity, several of which that will—if passed—eliminate the disparity altogether.

The authors of the viewpoints presented in *Opposing Viewpoints: Mandatory Minimum Sentencing* debate many of these issues in the following chapters: Does Mandatory Minimum Sentencing Alleviate Crime? Is Mandatory Minimum Sentencing Unfair? What Are the Effects of Mandatory Minimum Sentencing? and What Are Some Alternatives to Mandatory Minimum Sentencing? The information provided in this volume will provide insight into why mandatory sentencing has aroused so much controversy as well as the impact of mandatory minimum sentences on offenders, families, communities, and the court system.

Chapter 1

Does Mandatory Minimum Sentencing Alleviate Crime?

Chapter Preface

In the 1990s legislators, victims groups, and criminal justice organizations became frustrated at the level of violent crime and what they believed were too-lenient sentences for hardened criminals. A lot of blame was placed on judges and juries, whom critics felt were letting dangerous criminals off with sentences that did not fit the serious natures of the crimes. In some instances, the same crime received disparate sentences from different judges. Determined to pass tough-on-crime measures and implement standard sentences in order to eliminate wildly varied sentences for the same offense, state governments began to pass controversial three-strikes laws, which aimed to alleviate crime and protect innocent citizens. Three-strikes laws are statutes enacted by state governments that require the state courts to hand down a mandatory extended jail sentence to offenders who have been convicted of three serious criminal offenses.

The first to pass a three-strikes law was the state of Washington, whose law came into effect in 1993. A year later, California passed the most stringent three-strikes law in the nation. Known as Proposition 184, the "Three Strikes and You're Out" law ruled that a third felony conviction for any offense required the offender to serve a twenty-five-years-to-life mandatory prison term. This means that even if the third conviction, or "strike," is a nonviolent felony such as certain shoplifting arrests, the defendant must be sentenced to at least twenty-five years in prison. The three-strikes law quickly spread to other states. By 2004 twenty-six states and the federal government adopted versions of the three-strikes law—although none as harsh as California's controversial measure.

Almost immediately, charges that the three-strikes laws were unfair arose among critics and experts in the criminal justice field. As important were criticisms that the laws did not work—or at least, did not work as they were envisioned. For example, a study of California's three-strikes law showed that instead of alleviating crime, it encouraged more violent crimes. It was also reported that the law resulted in an exodus of serious criminals to neighboring states. Early studies of three-strikes laws found negligible impacts on overall recidivism rates among the general population. Other studies, however, showed a clear drop in California's crime rate since the implementation of the stringent law.

The viewpoints in the following chapter investigate the efficacy of mandatory minimum sentences and debate whether these laws truly alleviate crime or just create new problems in the communities they are designed to help.

Viewpoint 1

> *"Mandatory sentencing schemes . . . have been a significant factor in the reduction of violent crime over the last 30 years."*

Federally Mandated Minimum Sentences Alleviate Crime

J. Randy Forbes

J. Randy Forbes is a U.S. representative from Virginia and a member of the House Committee on the Judiciary. In the following viewpoint taken from congressional testimony, Forbes argues that mandatory minimum sentencing ensures a consistency in sentencing and eliminates the enormous disparity in sentencing that existed when the federal courts had sentencing discretion. Forbes also contends that mandatory sentences have alleviated crime by incapacitating repeat offenders and deterring others from committing crimes.

As you read, consider the following questions:

1. According to the author, how do mandatory minimum penalties promote public safety?

J. Randy Forbes, "Mandatory Minimum Sentencing: The Issues," Hearing Before the Subcommittee on Crime, Terrorism, and Homeland Security of the Committee of the Judiciary, House of Representatives, June 26, 2007.

2. According to Forbes, what did Senator Ted Kennedy call sentencing disparity?
3. Why does the author believe mandatory minimum sentencing helps prosecutors?

Mandatory minimum penalties are an effective means to ensure consistency in sentencing and to promote the public safety by deterring others from committing crimes and preventing recidivism [relapse into crime]. The need for mandatory minimum penalties has taken on a greater significance given the advisory nature of the Federal sentencing guidelines. The Supreme Court's 2005 decision in *United States v. Booker* invalidated the mandatory sentencing requirement of the sentencing guidelines. The U.S. Sentencing Commission's March 13, 2006, report on *Booker*'s impact identified substantial concerns about unrestrained judicial discretion. Such discretion undermines the very purpose of the Sentencing Reform Act to provide certainty and fairness in meeting the purposes of sentencing and avoiding unwarranted sentencing disparities among defendants with similar records who have been found guilty of similar criminal conduct.

The Sentencing Commission's data updated through the second quarter of 2007 shows continuing sentencing disparities, including a steady rate of nongovernment-sponsored below-guideline sentences for defendants; geographic disparities among the judicial circuits; and sentencing reductions in a significant number of drug-trafficking cases, immigration cases, firearms offenses, pornography and prostitution offenses and white collar [crimes]. Advisory sentencing guidelines that result in lower penalties for the worst offenders only increase the significance of mandatory minimum sentences.

Sentencing Discretion

Beginning in 1984, Democrat Congresses passed important mandatory minimums, along with other sentencing reforms,

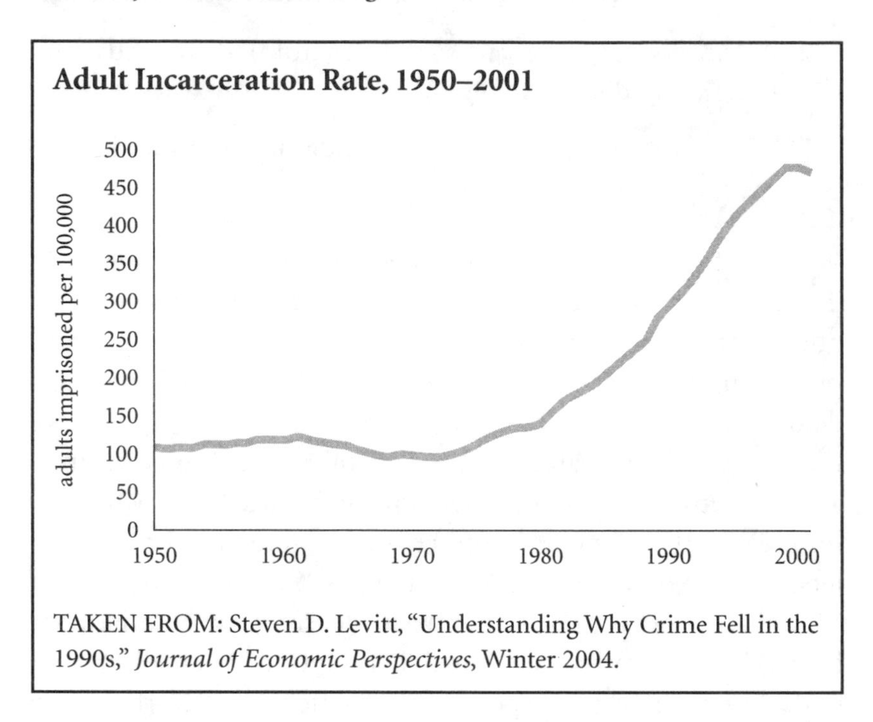

Adult Incarceration Rate, 1950–2001

TAKEN FROM: Steven D. Levitt, "Understanding Why Crime Fell in the 1990s," *Journal of Economic Perspectives*, Winter 2004.

including the Federal sentencing guidelines. Prior to the 1984 Sentencing Reform Act, Federal judges had unfettered discretion to sentence a criminal defendant as they pleased. This unbridled discretion resulted in enormous disparity in sentences for similarly situated defendants. Senator [Ted] Kennedy, one of the principal advocates of the Federal sentencing guidelines, stated that the existing sentencing disparity was a national scandal. He noted that the Federal Criminal Code invites disparity by conferring unlimited discretion on the sentencing judge.

The shameful disparity in criminal sentences imposed in the Federal courts is a major flaw which encourages the potential criminal to play the odds and beat the sentence. Sentencing disparity is unfair. Aside from ensuring consistency in sentencing, mandatory minimum penalties provide prosecutors the tools to secure the cooperation of criminals to dismantle criminal enterprises, gangs and other organizations. Without such a penalty, for example, gang members will not cooperate with law enforcement. They will simply turn their back on cooperation, do the time, and gang violence will continue to expand and threaten our communities.

Mandatory Sentences Work

While some complain about mandatory sentencing schemes there is research to show that such penalties have been a significant factor in the reduction of violent crime over the last 30 years. Some would say that is coincidence. Statistical researchers have shown to the contrary. Increases in prison population have incapacitated recidivists and deterred others from committing crime. Professor Steven Levitt conducted a study to show that a significant part of the decline in violent crime is attributable to increased incarceration. In a more recent study, Joanna Shepherd demonstrated that truth-in-sentencing laws have a dramatic impact on reducing serious violent crimes. Other studies confirmed the obvious point. Incarcerating an offender prevents him from repeating his crimes while he is in prison.

Balanced against these reductions in crime from deterrence and incapacity, there is significant cost savings to society from reducing the occurrence of crime.

VIEWPOINT 2

> *"Essentially we are looking at perhaps 1 or 2 percent of all the convictions involving Federal mandatory penalties."*

Federally Mandated Minimum Sentences Do Not Alleviate Crime

Marc Mauer

Marc Mauer is the executive director of The Sentencing Project, a national organization that advocates reforms in sentencing laws and practice. In the following viewpoint taken from congressional testimony, Mauer contends that federally mandated minimum sentences are based on false premises about their effectiveness in alleviating crime, that mandatory sentences have not reduced crime, and that alternative policies would work better than mandatory minimums.

As you read, consider the following questions:

1. According to the author, what did a 1991 Sentencing Commission report on mandatory sentencing show about plea negotiations?

Marc Mauer, "Congressional Testimony: Mandatory Minimum Sentencing: The Issues," Hearing Before the Subcommittee on Crime, Terrorism, and Homeland Security of the Committee of the Judiciary, House of Representatives, June 26, 2007. Reproduced by permission of the author.

2. What does Mauer say that studies show about the certainty of punishment rather than the severity of punishment?

3. What percentage of people prosecuted for crack cocaine offenses are low-level offenders, according to Sentencing Commission data cited by the author?

I want to address three key themes that address Federal mandatory sentencing, and these are, first, that the Federal mandatory penalties adopted in the 1980s were essentially based on false premises about their ability to reduce crime; secondly, mandatory sentencing has not, in fact, achieved its stated objectives; and thirdly, that alternative policies could produce more fair and more effective sentencing.

False Premises

Now, the first theme is that mandatory sentencing was based on false premises. Mandatory sentencing, as we have learned through many years, is not, in fact, mandatory; it is not, in fact, consistent. As far back as 1991, in the report by the Sentencing Commission, a comprehensive report on mandatory sentencing, we learned that in about a third of the cases that a mandatory sentence might have applied, in fact, the defendant was permitted to plead to a charge below the mandatory sentence. Now, there are a variety of reasons why that took place. There are also racial and ethnic disparities that resulted from those plea negotiations. But in terms of mandatory sentencing, somehow sending a message that if you do the crime, you do the time, we know that in a third of the cases that was not the case. These people went to prison, but for varying degrees of time.

Not an Effective Deterrent

Mandatory sentencing is also premised or has also been promoted as having a strong deterrent effect on potential offenders. And here I think we have a very serious problem in that

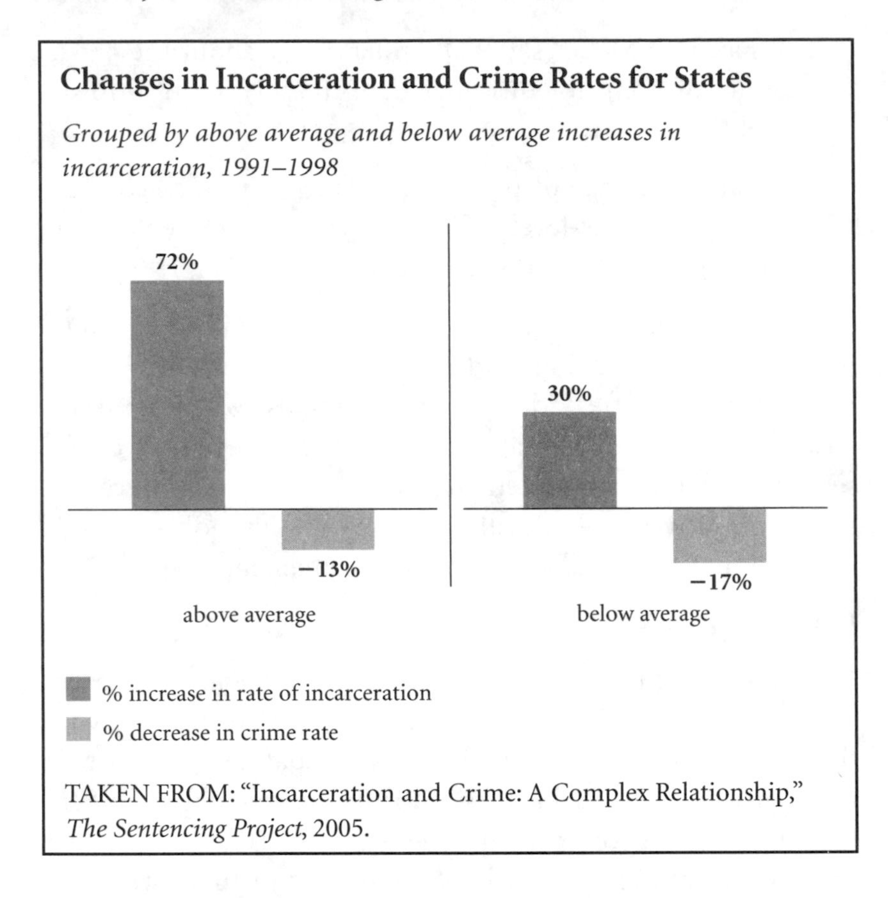

TAKEN FROM: "Incarceration and Crime: A Complex Relationship," *The Sentencing Project*, 2005.

the research on deterrence in criminal penalties for a very long period of time has shown us that deterrence is much more a function of the certainty of punishment rather than the severity of punishment. In other words, if a person believes that he or she will be caught for a crime, if there is more law enforcement out there or something like that, then he or she may think twice about committing a crime. But merely increasing the amount of punishment that someone is subject to for people who generally do not believe they will be caught does not add very much to any kind of deterrent value.

Mandatory Sentences and Drug Crimes

We see the mandatory penalties, as we know, in the Federal system have been overwhelmingly applied to drug offenses.

This is the area where they are also least likely to be effective, and that is because drug offenders, low-level sellers on the street, are easily replaced. As soon as we snatch up a few on the street corner, there is an almost endless supply, as we have seen through the war on drugs and the record number of arrests and incarcerations and an endless supply of people who are willing to take their place for a chance to make a quick buck or so. And so their replacement, in fact, diminishes any impact that the mandatories may have.

In terms of the level of success, we now have 20 years of experience with Federal mandatory penalties. Some proponents claim that the decline in crime in the 1990s is evidence of the success of mandatory penalties in particular. If we look at the research to date on why crime declined in the 1990s, the best research seems to suggest that at most about 25 percent of the decline in violent crime was due to rising incarceration. Some researchers believe it is as little as 10 or 15 percent. But we are talking here about incarceration in general. Of all the convictions in the U.S. every year, approximately 1 million, only 6 percent take place in Federal court. Of those, only a small fraction are mandatory penalties. So essentially we are looking at perhaps 1 or 2 percent of all the convictions involving Federal mandatory penalties. It is possible that has had an effect on crime, but we certainly have no idea from any of the research or any of the data, so it is extremely speculative to assume that that is a factor there.

Secondly, in terms of the level of success, as we have heard very clearly from the Sentencing Commission and many others, the drug quantity levels established in mandatory penalties, particularly for crack cocaine, not only are not effective but they encourage prosecution of lower-level offenders by setting the crack cocaine threshold at 5 grams. The Sentencing Commission data shows us that more than 60 percent of the people prosecuted for crack cocaine offenses are low-level offenders. This is not exactly what Federal resources should be doing, and we have seen as well, of course, the disproportionate impact on communities of color.

Thirdly what can we do to develop more effective and more fair sentencing policies? Well, since the [*United States v.*] *Booker* decision by the Supreme Court, we now have an even greater chasm between mandatory penalties, particularly for drugs, and all other Federal crimes. The sort of disruption in the sentencing grid or the sentencing proportions is even greater now that Federal judges have more discretion in non-mandatory cases. And it calls into question the whole structure much more severely.

Recommendations

What can we do? It seems to me Congress might want to request that the Sentencing Commission conduct an updated assessment of mandatory penalties. It has been 16 years now since the Sentencing Commission first did that.

Secondly, we want to review the drug quantities, particularly for crack cocaine, and raise that to the level of powder cocaine certainly.

It seems to me we should consider the expansion of the safety valve. This is used in approximately a third of the relevant drug cases. Judges are finding significant numbers of cases where it is appropriate. It may be time to see if judges should have more discretion in this regard as well.

Finally we see that the experience in the States over the last several years is one that is very much moving toward reform, reconsideration of sentencing policies. I think we have much to learn from that experience in the States. I think the States are moving in an interesting direction that suggests that maybe it is time to reconsider some of these policies.

Viewpoint 3

> *"Since California enacted its three strikes law in 1994, crime has dropped 26.9 percent."*

California's "Three Strikes" Law Alleviates Crime

Naomi Harlin Goodno

Naomi Harlin Goodno is an assistant professor at Pepperdine University School of Law. In the following essay, Goodno assesses the impact of California's "three strikes" law over its first ten years and concludes that it has proved effective by incapacitating violent criminals and providing a strong deterrence to crime. Goodno notes that California's crime rate has dropped significantly without substantially increasing state costs or overcrowding prisons.

As you read, consider the following questions:

1. What percentage of voters approved Proposition 184 in 1994, according to Goodno?
2. According to the author, under what circumstances does the "three strikes" provision take effect?

Naomi Harlin Goodno, "Career Criminals Targeted: The Verdict Is In, California's Three Strikes Law Proves Effective," *Golden Gate University Law Review*, vol. 37, 2006–2007.

3. What are the three reasons Goodno cites to prove that the "three strikes" law is effective?

Cladius Johnson is no stranger to crime. In 1979 he was convicted of gang rape. In 1985 he punched a woman in the face and stole her purse. In 1988 he was sentenced to 16 months for carrying an automatic machine gun. Had California's Three Strikes law been in effect, he could have received a sentence of 25 years to life. Instead, he was released and in 1989 he assaulted a woman with a deadly weapon. In 1995 he strangled and beat his wife into unconsciousness. Under California's Three Strikes law, he received a sentence of 25 years to life for this last crime. Johnson's story is not unique; there are other career criminals like him who committed crime after crime until California's Three Strikes law removed them from circulation.

Since its inception, California's Three Strikes law has generated controversy. Aimed at incarcerating career criminals, it has been tagged as one of the toughest "tough on crime" statutes in the country. Has it been effective? Supporters say yes and point to individuals like Johnson, a criminal recidivist [repeat offender] who is serving a long prison sentence. Opponents say no and argue that the law is overbroad because it hands down 25-years-to-life sentences for minor offenses like shoplifting a few videos or stealing golf clubs.

This article reviews the impact of the Three Strikes law over the last decade and concludes that, based on data that have been collected and the manner in which the law has been applied, it has proved effective. The first section of this article explores the history behind the legislation and the law itself. The second part of this article sets forth three reasons why the Three Strikes law has proved effective: (1) The Three Strikes law is carrying out its goals by incapacitating career criminals and deterring crime. Since its enactment, California's crime rate has dropped, and for the first time in 18 years, parolees are leaving the state. (2) Contrary to initial concerns, the Three Strikes law has been implemented without substantially increasing state costs or overcrowding prisons. (3) The Three Strikes law has built-in safeguards that allow trial judges and prosecutors to exercise discretion to ensure that the law targets those who are career criminals. This discretion has been successfully exercised throughout the state. This is evidenced by the fact that most incarcerated third-strikers who are serving sentences of 25 years to life committed more than three serious or violent felonies.

History of the Legislation

The murders of two young girls in the early 1990s raised California's public awareness of the problems associated with criminal recidivism. In 1992, 18-year-old Kimber Reynolds was murdered during an attempted purse snatching by a paroled felon whose criminal history included auto theft, gun, and drug charges. After her death, in April 1993, Kimber's father advocated for the first legislation aimed at increasing sentencing for recidivist criminals. He testified before the California Legislature in support of a bill adopting a three strikes sentencing structure that provided for sentences of 25 years to life in prison for certain recidivist offenders. However, the bill was unsuccessful.

Then, only a few months after the bill was struck down, 12-year-old Polly Klaas was kidnapped out of her home and murdered. Polly's murderer was also a career criminal who had been convicted of sexual assault, kidnapping, and burglary. Polly's murder brought the issues of the Three Strikes law to the public and political forefront.

By March 1994, the Legislature passed the Three Strikes bill by a large majority. It was signed into law and codified in California Penal Code sections 667(b)–(i). That same month, Kimber's father spearheaded a three strikes initiative (Proposition 184) gathering over 800,000 signatures. In November of the same year, California voters approved Proposi-

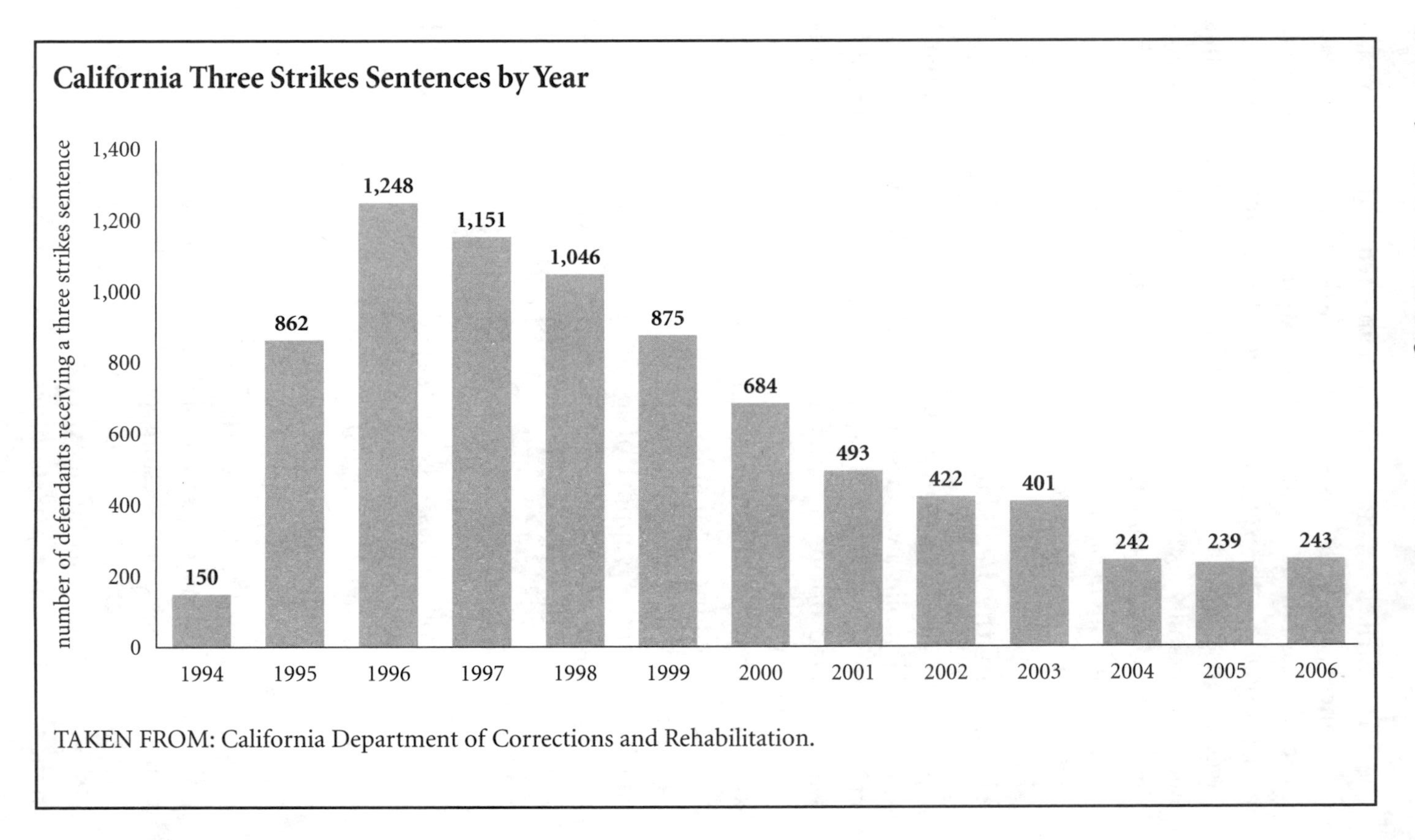

TAKEN FROM: California Department of Corrections and Rehabilitation.

tion 184 by 72 percent. The new law was codified in California Penal Code section 1170.12. The approved ballot initiative, which is "virtually identical" to section 667, can only be amended or repealed by a new ballot measure or by two-thirds vote of the Legislature.

Intent of the Law

According to section 667, the purpose of the Three Strikes law is "to ensure longer prison sentences and greater punishment for those who commit a felony and have been previously convicted of serious and/or violent felony offenses." The courts have specifically determined that the Three Strikes law is the articulation of a parallel sentencing scheme for specifically described recidivists, and is not an enhancement law. As Justice James A. Ardaiz of the Fifth Appellate District of California explained: "Three Strikes was intended to go beyond simply making sentences tougher. It was intended to be a focused effort to create a sentencing policy that would use the judicial system to reduce serious and violent crime." The focus of the law, therefore, is on the defendant's conduct—namely whether the defendant has failed to obey the law in the past.

Two Provisions

Although commonly referred to as the Three Strikes law, section 667 increases sentencing for career criminals with a two-strikes and a three-strikes provision. For the two-strikes provision to take effect, the prosecutor must prove beyond a reasonable doubt that the defendant had at least one prior serious or violent felony. Under the two-strikes provision, the court must double the sentence of the felony charged.

For the three-strikes provision to take effect, the prosecutor must prove beyond a reasonable doubt that the defendant had at least two prior serious or violent felonies. Under the three-strikes provision, the court must impose a sentence of at least 25 years to life.

Prior-Felony Requirement

For either provision to be triggered, the defendant must have been convicted of a "serious or violent felony." A serious or violent felony includes such crimes as murder, rape, robbery, kidnapping, and carjacking. Prior convictions count, regardless of when they occurred, and regardless of whether they occur out-of-state, so long as the conviction would be an equivalent offense in California.

Although the prior felony has to be serious or violent, the current felony charged does not. It is this last provision of the statute that has caused much controversy over California's Three Strikes law. While many other states and the federal government have sentencing statutes aimed at career criminals similar to Three Strikes, most of these laws require that the final strike also be a serious or violent felony.

Why the Law Is Effective

The Three Strikes law has been in effect for more than 10 years. Enough time has therefore passed for data to be collected and for the law to undergo legal challenges. As set forth in this section, a study of the Three Strikes law since its enactment reveals there are three main reasons why it has been effective: (1) the Three Strikes law appears to be meeting its theoretical goals; (2) some of the initial concerns of the impact of the law have not occurred; and (3) the interpretation of the law has provided for built-in safeguards to ensure that the intent of the law is carried out.

Theoretical Goals Being Met

There are at least two theoretical reasons that support the legislative intent of California's Three Strikes law. First, supporters of the law believed it would have an incapacitation effect. This means that repeat offenders would be jailed for longer periods of time, during which they would be incapable of committing new crimes. Second, supporters of the law believed it would have a deterrent effect, meaning that possible offenders would be deterred from committing crimes because of the potential for harsher sentences under the Three Strikes law. The statistics of the last decade imply that the Three Strikes law has had both an incapacitation and deterrent effect.

Incapacitation Effect. One observation that suggests that the Three Strikes law has had an incapacitation effect is that the number of sentenced third-strikers declined every year from 1996 through 2003. A similar decline occurred with second-strikers. Indeed, some claim that the drop in capital sentences since 2000 may be linked to the Three Strikes law. One possible interpretation of this decline is that there are fewer strikers every year because the law is doing its job. In other words, defendants who are habitual offenders are incapacitated and cannot commit any additional crimes while serving the longer sentence.

Moreover, inmates who are strikers have more serious criminal histories than non-strikers. While this may seem obvious in that the Three Strikes law is aimed at habitual offenders, this fact is important because it again shows that the law is doing what it should. It is incapacitating felons who, based on their criminal history, are generally more likely than others to commit crimes.

Deterrent Effect. Data also suggest that the Three Strikes law has had a deterrent effect. Specifically, California's crime rate has decreased since the law was enacted in 1994. A 1999 FBI study determined that "[s]ince California enacted its three strikes law in 1994, crime has dropped 26.9 percent, which translates to 815,000 fewer crimes." While numerous social and economic factors underlie crime rates, the correlation between the drop in California's crime rate and the enactment of the Three Strikes law is notable. One interpretation of this correlation is that potential offenders may be deterred from committing crimes because of the possibility of serving longer sentences.

In fact, several studies and surveys have concluded that the Three Strikes law has had a deterrent effect. For example, in one survey, a majority of juvenile offenders said that if they knew that they would receive 25 years to life in prison they would not commit a serious or violent felony. A more recent study determined the Three Strikes law has had a deterrent effect because it "reduces felony arrests rates among the class of criminals with 1 strike by 29 to 48 percent . . . and among the class of criminals with 2 strikes by 12.5 percent." Using an economic model, another study concluded that the Three Strikes law is actively deterring offenders from engaging in any criminal activity that would qualify as a first strike.

On another front, parole statistics also imply that the Three Strikes law has had a deterrent effect. Since the Three Strikes law was enacted, generally more parolees have left California than have come into the state. In the plurality opinion of *Ewing v. California*, United States Supreme Court Justice O'Connor noted this trend: "[a]n unintended but positive consequence of 'Three Strikes' has been the impact on parolees leaving the state. More California parolees are now leaving the state than parolees from other jurisdictions entering California. This striking turnaround started in 1994." This could suggest that parolees who are career criminals leave the state because they fear a harsher sentence if they commit additional felonies.

The Three Strikes law brought about another interesting change related to parolees. In 2000, the California Department of Corrections changed how it supervised parolees who are second-strikers (meaning that their next felony could make them third-strikers because they already have two serious or violent felony convictions). Certain parole agents who have lighter caseloads are specially trained to work with second-strikers. As of March 2005, there were approximately 12,000 second-striker parolees under this specialized supervision. While the data is scant as to whether this specialized parole supervision deters crime, logically, it seems that the parole system is taking an extremely active role in working with second-strikers to discourage them from committing any further felonies.

Some critics of Three Strikes cite this specialized parole as costing California approximately $20 million annually. Based on this number, the average yearly cost to the state per parolee is about $1,700. In comparison, however, the average yearly cost to the state per inmate is $34,150. Thus, it costs approximately 20 times more every year to jail an offender than to keep a second-striker under specialized parole. Given the enormous disparity between these costs, it seems likely that the program, even if it is only moderately successful, makes economic sense, not to mention the positive impact it has on preventing the human suffering of the would-be crime victim.

VIEWPOINT 4

> *"In general, arrests of three-strike-eligible felons are 20 percent more likely to be [for] violent crimes."*

California's "Three Strikes" Law Increases Violent Crime

Ray Fisman

Ray Fisman is the Lambert Family Professor of Social Enterprise and research director of the Social Enterprise program at Columbia University Business School. In the following viewpoint, Fisman points out that recent studies have shown that one of the unintended consequences of California's "three strikes" law is that it may push criminals to commit more serious and more violent crimes. So although the law has had an effect on the likelihood of just-released criminals becoming repeat offenders, it has failed in its original intent to avert violent crimes by putting habitual criminals away for good.

As you read, consider the following questions:

1. According to the author, how did the Polly Klaas murder inspire California's "three strikes" law?
2. What is a "record-aggravating" offense, according to Fisman?

3. What percentage of arrests of three-strikes-eligible felons are more likely to be violent crimes, according to the author?

On Oct. 1, 1993, a man named Richard Allen Davis kidnapped 12-year-old Polly Klaas during a slumber party at her home in Petaluma, Calif. At the time, Davis was on parole after serving half of a 16-year sentence for a prior kidnapping and had accumulated a 25-year rap sheet with charges ranging from burglary to auto theft to public intoxication. Polly was found raped and murdered a couple of months later, and the public outcry that ensued led to the passage of a California law that mandated stiff prison sentences for convicted felons on their third offense. Davis had more than a dozen convictions when he abducted Polly Klaas.

New Findings

"Three-strikes" laws have now been enacted in 26 states, often with the stated purpose of keeping society safe from violent criminals like Richard Davis. But a new study released by the National Bureau of Economic Research finds that three-strikes laws like California's, while discouraging criminals from doing things like smoking pot or shoplifting, may push those who do continue in a life of crime to commit more violent offenses. The study's author, Radha Iyengar, argues that this is because under such laws, felons with a pair of strikes against them have little to lose (and often much to gain) by committing serious crimes rather than minor offenses.

Why would stiffer penalties increase violent crime? To understand this seeming paradox, you first need to understand the nature of California's three-strikes law. Not just any offense gets you a first strike. It must be a so-called "record-aggravating" offense, which includes violent crimes like assault and rape as well as serious nonviolent crimes such as burglary or drug sales to minors. But after strike one, strikes two and three can come from any felony, including minor offenses like possession of marijuana or even stealing golf clubs or videotapes. A third strike carries with it a mandatory sentence of at least 25 years in prison.

Unintended Consequences

Now, put yourself in the shoes of a two-strike criminal. The prospect of 25 years behind bars for a third offense is likely to give even a hardened criminal pause before he or she crosses the street against the lights. So we'd expect two-strike felons to commit fewer crimes. But suppose you've already decided to break the law—maybe you need to make a quick buck. Are you going to lift a few golf clubs from the local pro shop? Or are you going to hold up a bank? The potential haul from a bank robbery is obviously much greater, and the penalty is the same: Bank robbery will get you decades in the slammer, but if it's your third offense, so will shoplifting.

Even if you don't quite have the chutzpah [daring] to pull off a bank job, you still might end up committing a more violent crime if you're in a 0-2 hole. Let's say you opt for the golf club caper, but as you're making your getaway, you're cornered by a store security guard. Do you surrender quietly or pull out a gun? If strike three is looming, it's all the same to you whether you end up on trial for shoplifting or armed assault, so why not try to shoot your way out of an arrest?

Proponents of three-strikes laws point to declines across the board in crime rates in California during the 1990s, following the passage of the three-strikes law—including rates of violent crime. But crime was dropping around the country during that period, with explanations ranging from new policing tactics to the legalization of abortion. With so much going on, it's hard to know how much, if any, of the decline comes from fear of a third strike. Instead of analyzing aggregate crime data, Iyengar looks at the lawbreaking choices of individual criminals. She examines how their lawbreaking activi-

"The problem with the Three Strikes Law is that they always go down swinging," cartoon by Jason Love. www.CartoonStock.com.

ties change when the three-strikes law is on the books and also how their lawbreaking activities change depending on how many strikes they have against them.

Some Good News

Using data from all criminal convictions during 1990 through 1999 in California's three biggest cities—Los Angeles, San Francisco, and San Diego—Iyengar finds that the three-strikes law did indeed have a large effect on the likelihood of recidivating (committing a crime after release from prison) in the two years following a prior offense. For those with one strike, the law reduced recidivism by 14 percent; this doubled to a 28 percent reduction for two-strikers, whose next crime would trigger the minimum 25-year prison term.

But that's where the good news ends. Three-strike-eligible criminals who actually do get arrested for a third offense commit more serious crimes. Burglars, for example, become robbers—these are both offenses that involve stealing, but robbery has the added element of force. Similarly, while thefts decline overall, assaults during thefts go up under three strikes, suggesting that an increasing number of thieves may, in desperation, be trying to muscle their way out of a third arrest (as in our golf club example). In general, arrests of three-strike-eligible felons are 20 percent more likely to be [for] violent crimes (relative to no-strike criminals).

(A Californian burglar on the verge of a third strike has an even safer option for his next act—take his activities out of state. Just across the border in Arizona, there's no three-strikes law at all, and in neighboring Nevada, the law is rarely invoked. So rather than breaking and entering in Los Angeles, why not take a road trip to Las Vegas or Phoenix instead? It seems that many criminals do. Iyengar finds that a larger fraction of repeat offenders recidivate out of state after the three-strikes law's passage.)

Well-Intentioned but Flawed

Overall, the three-strikes law did have the desired effect of deterring repeat offenders from striking again. But the law's original intent—motivated as it was by Polly Klaas' tragic story—was to avert further violent tragedies by putting habitual criminals away for a good, long time. It's putting away violent criminals, but Iyengar's study suggests it's also making criminals more violent. It's tempting to invoke the law of unintended consequences in thinking about what was perhaps a well-intentioned but flawed piece of legislation. But these consequences could have been entirely anticipated if legislators recognized that criminals, like all of us, often make decisions by rationally weighing the costs and benefits of their actions.

Viewpoint 5

> *"In drug cases, where the ultimate goal is to rid society of the entire trafficking enterprise, mandatory minimum statutes are especially significant."*

Mandatory Minimum Drug Sentences Help Alleviate Crime

Jodi L. Avergun

Jodi L. Avergun is the chief of staff of the Drug Enforcement Administration (DEA), a part of the U.S. Department of Justice. In the following testimony before a congressional subcommittee, she details the damage that drug trafficking and drug addiction has had on minors, which enforces the DEA's support of mandatory minimum sentences for drug offenses. She argues that the sentences are imperative for providing a level of uniformity and consistency in sentencing and offering a deterrent for those involved in illegal drug activity.

Jodi L. Avergun, "Defending America's Most Vulnerable: Safe Access to Drug Treatment and Child Protection Act of 2005," Hearing Before the Subcommittee on Crime, Terrorism, and Homeland Security of the Committee of the Judiciary, House of Representatives, April 12, 2005.

As you read, consider the following questions:

1. How many children were affected by clandestine drug laboratory–related incidents between 2000 and 2005, according to Avergun?
2. According to statistics maintained by the U.S. Sentencing Commission, and cited by the author, how many defendants per year were sentenced under the guideline that provided enhanced penalties for drug activity involving protected locations, minors or pregnant individuals between 1998 and 2002?
3. Why does Avergun believe that mandatory minimum sentences are particularly valuable for prosecutors?

The DEA has seen firsthand the devastation that illegal drugs cause in the lives of children. Children are our nation's future and our most precious resource, and, sadly, many of them are having their lives and dreams stolen by illegal drugs. This theft takes many forms, from a drug-addicted parent who neglects a child, to a clandestine methamphetamine "cook" using a child's play area as a laboratory site, to a parent using a child to serve as camouflage for their "stash," to a child being present during a drug transaction. The list goes on and on, but the end result remains the same: innocent children needlessly suffer from being exposed to illegal drugs.

The PROTECT Act

The Department of Justice and other law enforcement agencies at all levels seek to protect the most vulnerable segments of our society from those drug traffickers and drug addicted individuals who exploit those individuals least able to protect themselves. In 2003, Congress made significant strides in this area by enacting the Prosecutorial Remedies and Other Tools to end the Exploitation of Children Today Act, better known as the PROTECT Act. This law has proven effective in enabling law enforcement to pursue and to punish wrongdoers who threaten the youth of America. Last year [2003] Chairman [James] Sensenbrenner introduced H.R. 4547, the "Defending America's Most Vulnerable: Safe Access to Drug Treatment and Child Protection Act of 2004," which would have taken these efforts even further by focusing on the scourge of drug trafficking in some of its most base and dangerous forms: those who use minors to commit trafficking offenses, trafficking to minors, trafficking in places where minors are present, and trafficking in or near drug treatment centers.

Mr. Chairman, today my testimony is a follow-up to the testimony presented in July of last year to this Subcommittee by Ms. Catherine O'Neil, Associate Deputy Attorney General, regarding H.R. 4547. We request that her earlier testimony be made part of today's hearing record. We are here today to reiterate our support for legislation that addresses drug-related incidents involving minors.

Specific Cases of Drug Activity

The endangerment of children through exposure to drug activity, sales of drugs to children, the use of minors in drug trafficking, and the peddling of pharmaceutical and other illicit drugs to drug treatment patients are all significant problems today. Sadly, the horrific examples below are just a few instances where children have been found victimized and exploited by people whose lives have been taken over by drugs:

- From FY [fiscal year] 2000 through the first quarter of FY 2005, over 15,000 children were reported as being affected in clandestine laboratory-related incidents. The term "affected children" is defined as a child being present and/or evidence that a child lived at a clandestine laboratory site. This total reflects only those instances where law enforcement was involved. The true number of children affected by clandestine laboratory incidents is unknown, though it is surely much greater.

- In 2004, a defendant from Iowa pled guilty to conspiring to manufacture methamphetamine. Although the meth was not manufactured in the defendant's home, where the defendant's 4-year-old son also lived, it was used as the distribution point for large quantities of meth. The son's hair tested positive for extremely high levels of meth, indicating chronic exposure to the drug. In this case, no enhancement could be applied because of the son's exposure, as he had not been endangered during the actual manufacture of the meth.
- In November 2004, the DEA raided a suspected methamphetamine lab located in a home in Missouri. During this operation three children, all under five years of age, were found sleeping on chemical-soaked rugs. The residence was filled with insects and rodents and had no electricity or running water. Two guard dogs kept by the "cooks" to fend off law enforcement were also found: clean, healthy, and well-fed. The dogs actually ate off a dinner plate.

Currently, investigations targeting individuals involved in the manufacture of methamphetamine or amphetamine which are prosecuted on a federal level have a sentencing enhancement available. This enhancement provides a six-level increase and a guidelines floor at level 30 (about 8 to 10 years for a first offender) when a substantial risk of harm to the life of a minor or an incompetent individual is created. Unfortunately, investigations targeting traffickers involved in the distribution of other illegal drugs, such as heroin or cocaine, do not have this same enhancement. For example:

- During October 1999, the DEA's Philadelphia Field Division initiated a heroin investigation targeting an international organization ranging from street-level dealers and couriers to a source of supply in South America. This investigation resulted in "spin-off" investigations in New York and South America. Indictments and arrests stemming from the Philadelphia portion of this investigation began in early 2001, and resulted in over 20 arrests. The most significant charge filed against these defendants was Conspiracy to Distribute Heroin. Additionally, seven subjects were charged with Distribution of Heroin within 1,000 feet of a School.

- During August 2003, fire department personnel and local law enforcement authorities responded to a hotel fire in a family resort in Emmett County, Michigan. The fire was the result of a subject's attempts to manufacture methcathinone. Authorities subsequently seized a small quantity of methcathinone, along with chemistry books, from the room.
- In an investigation initiated by DEA's Philadelphia Field Division, a subject hid approximately 400 grams of heroin under his infant during a buy/bust operation. During the course of his guilty plea in March 2004, the defendant admitted that he stored the drugs under the infant.

Drug Prosecutions

The Department of Justice is committed to vigorously prosecuting drug trafficking in all of its egregious forms. Prosecutions range from high-level international drug traffickers to street-level predators who are tempting children or addicts with the lure of profit and the promise of intoxication.

We have had some successes. Statistics maintained by the U.S. Sentencing Commission indicate that between 1998 and 2002 over 300 defendants were sentenced annually under the guideline that provides for enhanced penalties for drug activity involving protected locations, minors, or pregnant indi-

Need for Strong Penalties

On September 11, 2001, America was attacked by terrorists based in foreign lands. This attack resulted in the murder of almost 3,000 Americans. Because of the intensity and magnitude of that single attack, it is easy to lose sight of the chemical attack that occurs daily in cities and towns in every state in the nation. Illegal drugs and their effects kill more than 19,000 Americans annually, and the impact on our economy is estimated to be more than $160 billion each year.

This continuous and unrelenting attack by international drug cartels, American street gangs, meth cookers, and neighborhood drug traffickers is equivalent to a September 11th tragedy every two months. We must continue our commitment to fighting these criminals as aggressively as we fight terrorists who have political motives. Tough drug laws such as those proposed in the "Safe Access to Treatment and Child Protection Act of 2005" are essential weapons in our arsenal.

Vigorous enforcement of drug laws helps to keep families and neighborhoods safe from violent criminals and serves as a deterrent to first-time drug use for most young people. It also helps many addicts reach the road to recovery through drug courts and other corrections-based treatment programs.

Ronald E. Brooks,
Testimony Before the Subcommittee on Crime, Terrorism, and Homeland Security, April 12, 2005.

viduals. But our tools are limited. And we have no specific weapon against those who distribute controlled substances within the vicinity of a drug treatment center.

The people who would sink to the depths of inhumanity by targeting their trafficking activity at those with the least ability to resist such offers are deserving of the most severe punishment. The Department of Justice cannot and will not tolerate this conduct in a free and safe America, and that is why the Department of Justice stands firmly behind the intent of this legislation to increase the punishment meted out to those who would harm us, our children, and those seeking to escape the cycle of addiction.

Mandatory Minimum Sentences

The Department of Justice supports mandatory minimum sentences in appropriate circumstances. In a way sentencing guidelines cannot, mandatory minimum statutes provide a level of uniformity and predictability in sentencing. They deter certain types of criminal behavior determined by Congress to be sufficiently egregious as to merit harsh penalties by clearly forewarning the potential offender and the public at large of the minimum potential consequences of committing such an offense. And mandatory minimum sentences can also incapacitate dangerous offenders for long periods of time, thereby increasing public safety. Equally important, mandatory minimum sentences provide an indispensable tool for prosecutors, because they provide the strongest incentive to defendants to cooperate against the others who were involved in their criminal activity.

In drug cases, where the ultimate goal is to rid society of the entire trafficking enterprise, mandatory minimum statutes are especially significant. Unlike a bank robbery, for which a bank teller or an ordinary citizen could be a critical witness, often in drug cases the critical witnesses are drug users and/or other drug traffickers. The offer of relief from a mandatory minimum sentence in exchange for truthful testimony allows the Government to move steadily and effectively up the chain of supply, using the lesser distributors to prosecute the more serious dealers and their leaders and suppliers. Mandatory minimum sentences are needed in appropriate circumstances, such as trafficking involving minors and trafficking in and around drug treatment centers.

> *"For far too long, the Federal [mandatory minimum drug] sentencing laws have created an injustice in our nation."*

Mandatory Minimum Drug Sentences Are Unjust

Patrick Leahy

Patrick Leahy is a U.S. senator from Vermont and the chairman of the Senate Committee on the Judiciary. In the following testimony at a congressional hearing on drug sentencing policy, he identifies the crack vs. powder cocaine sentencing disparity as a huge and ongoing problem in the American judicial system, deeming the mandatory minimum crack cocaine sentences unfair and flawed and not very effective in alleviating crime. Leahy suggests further reform of mandatory crack cocaine laws to make U.S. laws more effective and consistent with American values.

As you read, consider the following questions:

1. How does Leahy describe the effect that the mandatory minimum sentence for crack cocaine law has had on racial and ethnic minorities?

Patrick Leahy, "Restoring Fairness to Federal Sentencing," Subcommittee on Crime and Drugs, Committee on the Judiciary, April 29, 2009.

2. According to the author, how have mandatory minimum cocaine sentencing laws failed to do what they set out to do?
3. What did the Supreme Court rule in 2007 regarding the crack-powder disparity, according to Leahy?

Today [April 29, 2009] marks the 100th day of President Obama's administration, and already we have seen a response to the President's call for change. The Judiciary Committee today considers necessary changes and reforms in our Federal sentencing laws.

Our hearing will examine the unequal and unfair penalties for crack and powder cocaine offenses. We will consider how best to make our drug laws more fair, more rational, and more consistent with the core values of justice. The Committee has examined this issue before, in hearings in 2002 and, more recently, last year [in 2008].

I thank Senator [Dan] Durbin for holding this hearing in the Crime and Drugs Subcommittee. We must do all we can to restore public confidence in our criminal justice system, and I hope this hearing can be a positive step toward reaching that goal.

The Crack-Powder Cocaine Disparity

For more than 20 years, our nation has used a Federal cocaine sentencing policy that treats "crack" offenders one hundred times more harshly than cocaine offenders without any legitimate basis for the difference. We know that there is little or no pharmacological distinction between crack and powder cocaine, yet the resulting punishments for these offenses is radically different and the resulting impact on minorities has been particularly unjust.

Under this flawed policy, a first-time offender caught selling five grams of powder cocaine typically receives a six-month sentence, and would often be eligible for probation.

Racial/Ethnic Proportion of Regular Drug Users, 1999–2005

Year	White %	Black %	Hispanic %
1999	72.1	13.4	10.2
2000	74.8	11.5	9.1
2001	74.2	11.9	9.9
2002	71.8	13.3	10.7
2003	71.0	12.3	12.2
2004	70.7	12.7	11.7
2005	69.2	14.0	12.4

TAKEN FROM: Marc Mauer, "The Changing Racial Dynamics of the War on Drugs," *The Sentencing Project*, April 2009.

That same first-time offender selling the same amount of crack faces a mandatory five-year prison sentence, with little or no possibility of leniency. This policy is wrong and unfair, and it has needlessly swelled our prisons, wasting precious Federal resources.

Racial and Ethnic Disparities

Even more disturbingly, this policy has had a significantly disparate impact on racial and ethnic minorities. According to the latest statistics of the United States Sentencing Commission, African-American offenders continue to make up the majority of Federal crack cocaine trafficking offenders, accounting for 80 percent of all Federal crack cocaine offenses, compared to white offenders who account for just 10 percent. These statistics are startling. It is no wonder this policy has sparked a nationwide debate about racial bias and undermined our citizens' confidence in the justice system.

These penalties, which Congress created in the mid-1980s, have failed to address basic concerns. The primary goal was to punish the major traffickers and drug kingpins who were bringing crack into our neighborhoods. Many people were also concerned about the impact of the crack epidemic on young people in urban areas. But the law has not been used to go after the most serious offenders; in fact, just the opposite has happened. The Sentencing Commission has consistently reported for many years that over half of Federal crack cocaine offenders are low-level street dealers and users, not the major traffickers Congress intended to target.

Changing Attitudes

We revisit this issue at a time when attitudes are changing in our nation about sentencing policy. The Sentencing Commission's 2008 report to Congress made clear that the reasons that led Congress to adopt these penalties were flawed, and have not withstood the test of time. Many recent reports and studies have concluded that the 100-to-one ratio now in the law is scientifically flawed, and supported by no empirical evidence at all. These findings have been a driving force behind recent actions by the Sentencing Commission, and underlie the courts' efforts to begin fixing these unjust drug laws.

The Supreme Court of the United States ruled in 2007 that the Federal courts have the power to address the unfair crack-powder disparity in Federal sentencing laws in certain cases. Two years ago [in 2007], the Sentencing Commission voted to change the guidelines and reduce the sentences for crack offenders in order to begin righting this wrong in the context of the law. Unfortunately, the past administration [of George W. Bush] did not welcome these reforms.

In the last Congress, then–Attorney General Michael Mukasey testified before the House Judiciary Committee suggesting that thousands of violent gang members and dangerous drug offenders will be instantaneously and automatically set free in communities across the country. This was an effort to use fear and ignorance to oppose a reform supported by many Republicans and Democrats. Of course, no one can be released without a hearing before a Federal judge, who must evaluate a defendant's criminal history and propensity for violence before approving any release. And, as we will hear from Sentencing Commission Acting Chair, Judge Ricardo Hinojosa, nothing of the sort has happened. In fact, allowing those unfairly sentenced to be released has not led to a spike in crime, as predicted by former–Attorney General Mukasey, and the process, as supervised by the Judiciary, is proceeding smoothly and efficiently.

Reforms Are Welcome

These modest changes have been welcomed by Federal judges across the country, including an outstanding Federal judge who will testify today—the Honorable Reggie Walton. The changes are also consistent with the goals of the Sentencing Reform Act, which requires all judges to consider "the need to avoid unwarranted sentence disparities among defendants with similar records who have been found guilty of similar conduct" before imposing any sentence. These reforms have started to bring us closer to a more rational drug policy. These changes, however, have done nothing to address the core problem, which is the codification of the 100-to-one ratio in Federal law.

We have also heard bipartisan calls for cocaine sentencing reform in the Senate. In the Judiciary Committee, Senators [Orrin] Hatch, [Jeff] Sessions, and [John] Cornyn have supported reducing the current 100-to-one sentencing disparity to a 20-to-one ratio. Senator Hatch, who has called the current ratio "an unjustifiable disparity," recognizes that because "crack and powder cocaine are pharmacologically the same drug" our sentencing laws do "not warrant such an extreme disparity." Senator Sessions, a former Federal prosecutor, has said, "The 100-to-one disparity in sentencing between crack cocaine and powder cocaine is not justifiable. Our experience with the guidelines has convinced me that these changes will make the criminal justice system more effective and fair. It's time to act." Senator Cornyn, a former state Supreme Court judge and Attorney General, has said, "laws should be firm but fair. We not only need just laws, but they need the appearance and reality of fairness."

Bipartisan Calls for Reform

I am encouraged by these bipartisan calls for reform. It sends a strong message, from Senators on both sides of the aisle, that the 100-to-one sentencing disparity between crack and powder cocaine is unjust, the data supporting it was unsound, and our drug laws need correction.

More than a year before taking office, in September 2007, then-Senator Obama said:

> "If you are convicted of a crime involving drugs, of course you should be punished. But let's not make the punishment for crack cocaine that much more severe than the punishment for powder cocaine when the real difference is where the people are using them or who is using them."

I agree. For far too long, the Federal crack-powder sentencing laws have created an injustice in our nation. For more than 20 years this policy has contributed to the swelling of our prison population, disproportionately impacted African and Hispanic Americans, and wasted limited federal resources on low-level street dealers rather than on the worst offenders—the drug kingpins.

We must be smarter in our Federal drug sentencing policy, of course, law enforcement has been and continues to be central to combating the scourge of drugs, but we must also find meaningful, community-based solutions that address the underlying causes of these problems. Solving these problems as they arise is essential, but being able to prevent them is an important goal that would not only save time and effort, but large amounts of money in a time when budgets are tight.

Periodical Bibliography

The following articles have been selected to supplement the diverse views presented in this chapter.

Joe Domanick	"Prisoners of Panic," *Los Angeles Times*, January 6, 2008.
Theo Emery	"Will Crack-Cocaine Sentencing Reform Help Current Cons?" *Time*, August 7, 2009.
Bradford Plumer	"Two Lonely Senators Look at Prison Reform," *New Republic*, October 25, 2007.
Eli Sanders	"The Last Drug Czar," *American Prospect*, June 29, 2009.
Debra J. Saunders	"Escaping the Myth of 'Three Strikes' State Prison Law," *San Francisco Chronicle*, July 6, 2008.
Debra J. Saunders	"Huge Crack in System of Drug Prosecution," Townhall.com, May 7, 2009. http://townhall.com/columnists/DebraJSaunders/2009/05/07/huge_crack_in_system_of_drug_prosecution.
Charles Stimson	"A Crack-Job on Jail Sentences," Heritage Foundation Press Commentary, March 3, 2008. www.heritage.org/Press/Commentary/ed030308a.cfm.
Jacob Sullum	"Mind the Gap," *Reason*, December 19, 2007.
Jasmine Tyler and Anthony Papa	"An End to Crack/Powder Cocaine Sentencing Disparity," *Counterpunch*, April 3, 2009.
Katrina Vanden Heuvel	"Drop the Rock," *Nation*, February 19, 2009.

Chapter 2

Is Mandatory Minimum Sentencing Unfair?

Chapter Preface

One of the major concerns people have with mandatory minimum sentences is whether such laws are fair and just. Is it fair to sentence offenders to long incarceration periods in spite of what may be mitigating circumstances? Is it just to sentence low-level, nonviolent offenders to harsh sentences that were originally meant for violent criminals or drug kingpins? The inherent fairness of applying mandatory minimum sentences to every case—and ignoring facts of the case that might warrant mercy or consideration—has been a subject of vigorous and often heated debate in both state and federal agencies and institutions.

The controversial case of Leandro Andrade illustrates the problem many people have with mandatory minimum sentences. On November 4, 1995, Andrade stole five children's videotapes from a Kmart store in Ontario, California. A few days later, he was caught stealing four more videotapes from another Kmart store. Because of his extensive history of crime, including convictions for petty theft, burglary, and transportation of marijuana, Andrade was subject to California's stringent "three strikes" law, which means that offenders convicted of three felonies or more will be sentenced to a mandatory jail term of twenty-five-years-to-life. Because Andrade was charged with two felonies, he was sentenced to two twenty-five-year jail sentences.

Critics of the "three strikes" law and mandatory minimum sentences would ask the fundamental question: is that a just sentence for someone who stole a total of nine videotapes? Does the severe punishment really fit the crime? They assert that such harsh mandatory sentences violate the Eighth Amendment of the U.S. Constitution, which prohibits cruel and unusual punishment. In a review of the case, Supreme

Court justice Stephen Breyer noted that in most states, twenty-five-years-to-life is the sentence for first-degree murder, not shoplifting.

Defenders of mandatory minimum sentencing laws would note that Andrade is a recidivist offender with an extensive criminal history, and taking him off the street protects people and property. They would claim that mandatory minimum sentences protect the innocent and punish the guilty and are effective in reducing the crime rate.

The viewpoints in the following chapter debate the essential fairness of "three strikes" laws and the disparity between crack and powder cocaine mandatory minimum sentences, which have sparked controversy and efforts at sentencing reform in the past several years.

Viewpoint 1

> *"Taking discretion away from judges was supposed to make sentencing more uniform, and thus fairer, but that hasn't been the case for mandatory minimums."*

Mandatory Minimum Sentencing Is Unfair

Emily Bazelon

Emily Bazelon is a senior editor at Slate, *an online magazine. In the following viewpoint, she argues that although lawmakers once were eager to adopt mandatory minimum sentences because they would mean consistent sentences, mandatory minimums have actually resulted in unfair and inconsistent penalties because they give the balance of power to prosecutors, not judges. Bazelon contends that prosecutors use the threat of a mandatory jail sentence to get plea bargains, thereby ensuring that some criminals get long sentences and others do not.*

As you read, consider the following questions:

1. According to the author, how many separate federal mandatory minimum penalties existed in 1991?

2. Since the late 1980s, how has the number of federal prisoners changed according to Bazelon?
3. What is the U.S. incarceration rate in relation to that of England, France, Germany, and Italy, as cited by the author?

Weldon Angelos is one unlucky rap producer. In May and June 2002, the founder of Extravagant Records, which counts Snoop Dogg among its clients, twice sold $350 worth of pot to a Utah police informant. The first time Angelos carried a pistol in the center console of his car; the second time he had one in an ankle holster. When the police searched his apartment more than a year later, they found three handguns. Angelos wasn't accused of hurting or threatening anyone. He has no criminal record. But after he turned down a plea bargain that would have locked him up for 15 years, the irked federal prosecutors in Salt Lake City piled on three counts under the federal statute that penalizes drug dealers for carrying weapons. One count would have gotten Angelos five extra years in prison. Three of them got him 55. All told, Angelos faced a possible 61 years behind bars once the jury convicted him. He is 24 years old.

Paul Cassell, the presiding judge in Angelos' case, is a Bush II [that is, George W. Bush] appointee and an unlikely angel of mercy. As a law professor at the University of Utah, he crusaded to eliminate the *Miranda* warnings [given by police to arrestees informing them of their rights] (even though the cops weren't complaining about giving them) and went on television to defend the Texas courts when they rejected the appeal of a man who was sentenced to death after his lawyer slept during his trial. But even Cassell balked at sentencing nonviolent, first-time-offender Angelos to a virtual life sentence. He polled the jurors, who recommended an average sentence of 18 years. He then compiled a list of federal sentences for serious violent crimes and came up with num-

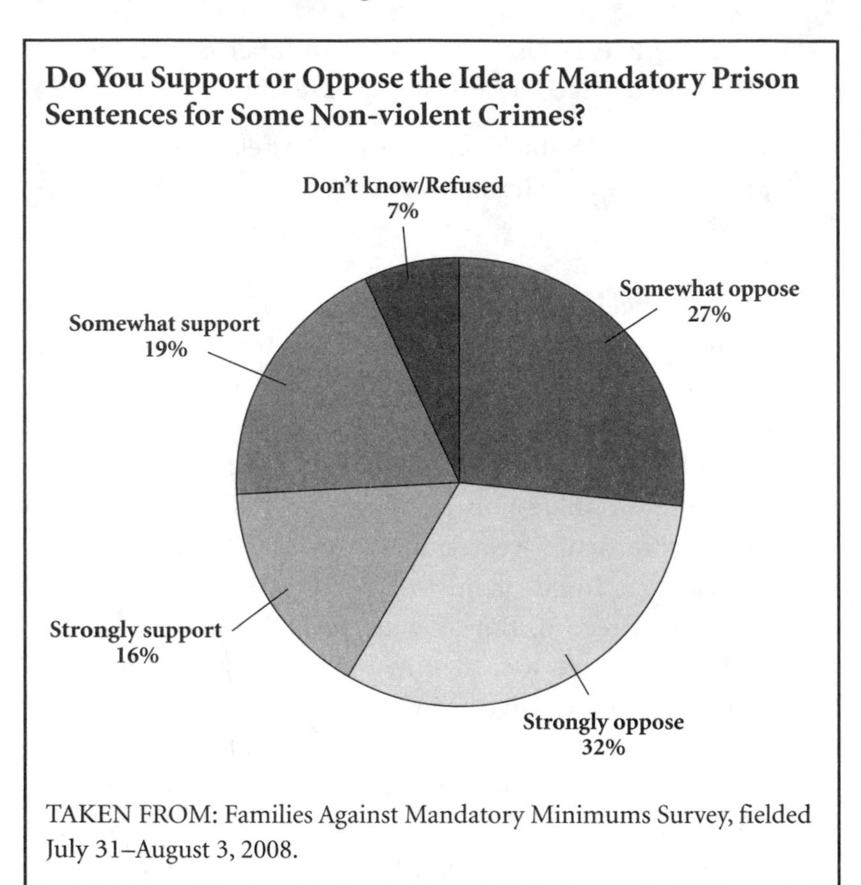

TAKEN FROM: Families Against Mandatory Minimums Survey, fielded July 31–August 3, 2008.

bers—like 24 years for an airplane hijacker, 19 years for a bomb-detonating terrorist, and 15 years for a three-time child rapist. Despite all his misgivings, however, Cassell bowed to the law and sentenced Weldon Angelos to 55 years and a day.

Judges Fed Up

"The court believes that to sentence Mr. Angelos to prison for the rest of his life is unjust, cruel, and even irrational," the judge wrote. "The court reluctantly concludes that it has no choice." In that grim sentiment, and Weldon Angelos' grim future, lay hundreds of thousands of wasted years and damaged lives. The federal courts are supposed to be a beacon of enlightenment for the far more burdened state system. Instead, thanks in large part to mandatory minimum sentencing, they've become a beacon of harshness. Lawmakers vote in droves for the automatic penalties because they make it easy to look tough on crime. But the sentences have become anathema [taboo] to federal judges across the ideological spectrum. Despite the outcome of Angelos' case, the judiciary is ready to revolt. And this year [2004], judges may finally give themselves the legal weapon they've been waiting for.

Congress fell in love with mandatory minimums—laws requiring anyone convicted of a given offense to receive a minimum penalty prescribed by legislation—during the drug epidemic of the 1980s. The punishments began as a way to declare war on dealers who sold crack or sold to minors, but they quickly became a way to declare war on just about anyone. By 1991, there were more than 100 separate mandatory-minimum penalties floating around the federal code. Thanks to those punishments, and the federal sentencing guidelines, since the late 1980s, the number of federal prisoners has more than quadrupled, and their average time served has doubled.

It's not the rising tide that bothers judges like Cassell, however. It's their utter lack of power to do anything for the exceptional defendants who move them. In August 2003, Supreme Court Justice Anthony Kennedy, another notorious unsoftie, railed against mandatory minimums in a speech to the American Bar Association. Kennedy pointed out that the United States' rate of incarceration is one in 143 people, compared to one in 1,000 in England, France, Germany, and Italy. He said that one in 10 African-American men in their mid- to late 20s are behind bars. And he noted that the cost of housing the prison population is more than $40 billion a year. But what really burned Kennedy was the way in which mandatory minimums shift critical decision-making power from judges to prosecutors. "A transfer of sentencing discretion from a judge to an assistant U.S. attorney, often not much older than the defendant, is misguided," the justice sniffed.

Mandatory Minimums Unfair

Taking discretion away from judges was supposed to make sentencing more uniform, and thus fairer, but that hasn't been the case for mandatory minimums. The U.S. Sentencing Commission, which monitors federal sentencing, found in 2000 that only 10 percent to 30 percent of drug offenders who carried or used a gun were penalized for doing so. Prosecutors charged the extra count only when it suited them. To them, mandatory minimums are the ace in the hole of plea bargaining. A defendant knows that if he turns down a plea offer, the prosecutor can add on charges that will put him away for a long, long time—never mind what the judge thinks.

While Kennedy's opposition to mandatory minimums is the consensus view among judges, the judiciary hasn't yet figured out how to get rid of the penalties. The Supreme Court has repeatedly rejected the obvious constitutional arguments against mandatory minimums—that they constitute cruel and unusual punishment or impose penalties that are disproportional to the crimes they are punishing. In Angelos' case, Judge Cassell said that he had to impose the 61-year sentence so long as there was a plausible basis for Congress to so instruct. Since Congress could have designed the punishment to deter drug dealers from carrying guns, the judge reasoned, he had to follow those legislative orders, however ham-fisted.

Possible Solutions

How to fix this? The solution may lie with *Blakely v. Washington*, [2003]'s Supreme Court ruling, which threw courts across the country into turmoil. In *Blakely*, the justices held the Washington state sentencing guidelines violated the Sixth Amendment—which guarantees the right to trial by jury—by increasing punishments based on facts found by a judge rather than jurors. The logic of *Blakely*, suggested that the federal guidelines would be the next to go, and that question is now before the high court in a pair of cases that were argued in

October [2004]. [In 2002], the Supreme Court rejected a Sixth Amendment challenge to federal mandatory minimums 5-4 in the case *United States v. Harris.* But if the justices throw over the federal guidelines, as some seem eager to do, the legal landscape would be altered, and mandatory minimums would be fair game again. And it would take only one switched vote to overturn *Harris.*

If the Supreme Court were to throw out mandatory minimums, the battle over sentencing between the courts and Congress would really be joined. Should federal judges go back to meting out individualized punishments? Can Congress come up with something better? That's a debate worth having. But in the meantime, it all offers small comfort to Weldon Angelos.

VIEWPOINT 2

> *"Federal sentencing guidelines have achieved the ambitious goals of public safety and fairness set out by Congress."*

Mandatory Minimum Sentencing Is Fair

Alberto Gonzales

Alberto Gonzales was the attorney general of the United States during the administration of President George W. Bush. In the following speech in front of a victims' rights group in Washington, D.C., he chronicles the origins of the Sentencing Reform Act of 1984 that implemented mandatory minimum sentences, claiming that the legislation aimed to ensure that those convicted of crimes serve tough and fair sentences. Gonzales bemoans the growing trend of allowing judges some discretion in sentencing, arguing that it "threatens the progress we have made in ensuring tough and fair sentences for federal offenders."

As you read, consider the following questions:

1. What did the *U.S. v. Booker* case hold for federal sentencing guidelines, according to the author?
2. What does Gonzales consider as a developing trend in the aftermath of the *Booker* case?

Alberto Gonzales, "Sentencing Guidelines," speech in Washington, D.C., June 21, 2005.

3. What were the two broad goals of the Sentencing Reform Act of 1984, in the author's opinion?

My wife, Rebecca, and I have a long-standing concern for the issues facing victims of crime. Becky spent three-and-a-half years in the Texas Attorney General's Office supporting sexual assault programs across the state. In my time with Governor [George W.] Bush in Texas, I spoke to many victims and their families in connection with clemency decisions made by the Governor. Together, Rebecca and I have met with hundreds of crime victims, heard their stories, and worked to protect their rights and ensure that their voices are heard.

We know from experience that there is nothing in the word "victim" that captures this movement, your commitment, your courage, and your passion.

True victimization requires the apathy of leaders, the silence of good people, and the hopelessness of the victims themselves.

The Victims' Rights Movement

But there is a wonderful metamorphosis at the heart of the victims' rights movement. From the ranks of the powerless has emerged a march of the empowered.

For decades, victims of crime lived in fear and suffered in silence. So-called experts told us that high levels of crime were inevitable, especially among the poor. The message to victims of crime—who were disproportionately poor as well—was inescapable: learn to live with it.

But thanks to the work of victims' groups and other concerned Americans, the status of victims of crime in America began to change. Victims, and their friends and loved ones, began to demand more from our system of justice.

Important policies designed to ensure the vindication of victims' rights in federal criminal cases have been developed during the Bush Administration. [In 2004], the President

Federal Mandatory Minimum Drug Sentences for First Convictions

Type of drug	Five years no parole	10 years no parole
Crack cocaine	5 grams	50 grams
Powder cocaine	500 grams	5 kilos
Heroin	100 grams	1 kilo
LSD	1 gram	10 grams
Marijuana	100 plants or 100 kilos	1000 plants or 1000 kilos
Methamphetamine	5 grams (pure)/50 grams (mixture)	50 grams (pure)/500 grams (mixture)
PCP	10 grams (pure)/100 grams (mixture)	100 grams (pure)/1 kilo (mixture)

Other mandatory minimum sentences

Offense	Length of sentence
Firearm possessed during drug offense	5 years added to drug sentence
Armed Career Criminal Act *(Felon in possession of a gun with three prior felony convictions)*	15 years
Continuing Criminal Enterprise	20 years

TAKEN FROM: Families Against Mandatory Minimums, 2008.

signed the Justice for All Act. I recently revised and reissued the Attorney General Guidelines for Victim and Witness Assistance.

Mandatory Minimum Sentences

For victims, another key aspect of any fair and equitable criminal justice system is to ensure that those convicted of crimes serve tough and fair sentences. And since 1987, we have had a sentencing system for federal offenses that responded to this demand—and has helped to achieve the lowest crime rates in a generation.

The key to this system was a set of mandatory sentencing guidelines that specified a range within which federal judges were bound to impose sentences, absent unusual circumstances. The guidelines reflected a careful balancing by Congress and the Sentencing Commission between discretion and consistency in sentencing. But the mandatory guidelines system is no longer in place today, and I believe its loss threatens the progress we have made in ensuring tough and fair sentences for federal offenders.

That threat is illustrated by the story of two defendants, both convicted of similar charges involving possession of child pornography, one in New York, the other across the Hudson River in New Jersey.

The New York defendant faced a sentencing range of 27 to 33 months in prison, but received only probation.

The New Jersey defendant faced a sentencing range of 30 to 37 months and was given a sentence of 41 months in prison.

What made the difference?

Flexible Sentencing Process

[In January 2005], the Supreme Court ruled that federal sentencing guidelines mandated by bipartisan congressional majorities in 1984 are advisory only and are no longer binding on federal judges.

In that case, *U.S. v. Booker*, the Court held that federal sentencing guidelines violated a defendant's rights under the Sixth Amendment of our Constitution. The result is that, today, judges must take the guidelines into account when sentencing, but are no longer bound by the law to impose a sentence within the range prescribed by the guidelines.

So in the New Jersey child pornography case, the judge deemed it necessary to protect the public from the defendant and imposed a sentence slightly above the guideline range. In the New York case, however, the judge reasoned that the defendant would benefit from continued psychological treatment and ordered probation only.

Developing Trend

The story of these two defendants is just one example that illustrates a developing trend in the aftermath of the *Booker* decision. More and more frequently, judges are exercising their discretion to impose sentences that depart from the carefully considered ranges developed by the U.S. Sentencing Commission. In the process, we risk losing a sentencing system that requires serious sentences for serious offenders and helps prevent disparate sentences for equally serious crimes.

A Need for Reform

And why, you may be asking, should victims and victims' groups be concerned about sentencing?

The federal sentencing guidelines were the result of Republicans and Democrats coming together in response to the high crime rates of the 1960s and 1970s to create an invaluable tool of justice.

As the rates of serious violent felonies more than tripled, a consensus emerged that society needed to be protected from the early release of offenders.

Also undermining Americans' faith in the system was the fact that significant disparities existed in the sentences received by individuals guilty of equally serious offenses.

A widespread and bipartisan consensus took hold that our system of sentencing was unfair and broken.

Sentencing Reform Act of 1984

So in 1984, lawmakers from across the political spectrum passed the Sentencing Reform Act with two broad goals in mind.

The first was to increase the safety of law-abiding Americans by restoring in sentencing an emphasis on punishment, incapacitation, and deterrence.

The second was to ensure fairness in sentencing. The statute's guiding principle was consistency—defendants who had committed equally serious crimes and had similar criminal backgrounds should receive similar sentences, irrespective of their race or the race of their victim and irrespective of geographic location or economic background.

In the 17-plus years that they have been in existence, federal sentencing guidelines have achieved the ambitious goals of public safety and fairness set out by Congress.

Mandatory Minimums Work

The United States is today experiencing crime rates that are the lowest in a generation. If crime rates during the last 10 years had been as high as the rates 30–40 years ago, then 34 million additional violent crimes would have been committed in the last decade.

Of course, no single law or policy is by itself responsible for today's low levels of violent crime. But multiple, independent studies of our criminal justice system confirm what our common sense tells us: increased incarceration means reduced crime, and federal and state sentencing reform has helped put the most violent, repeat offenders behind bars, and kept them there for sentences appropriate to their crimes.

Federal sentencing guidelines have helped keep Americans safe while also delivering on their promise to reduce unwarranted disparities in sentences. When the U.S. Sentencing Commission recently took stock of 15 years experience with the federal sentencing guidelines, it noted that studies by both the Commission itself and others have determined that the guidelines, quote, "have succeeded at the job they were principally designed to do: reduce unwarranted disparity arising from differences among judges."

For 17 years, mandatory federal sentencing guidelines have helped drive down crime. The guidelines have evolved over time to adapt to changing circumstances and a better understanding of societal problems and the criminal justice system. Judges, legislators, the Sentencing Commission, prosecutors, defense lawyers, and others have worked hard to develop a system of sentencing guidelines that has protected Americans and improved American justice.

Viewpoint 3

> *"On average, only 1 out of every 9 eligible third strikers gets a '25 to Life' sentence."*

California's "Three Strikes" Law Is Fair

Mike Reynolds

Mike Reynolds is the father of Kimber Reynolds, who was murdered in 1992 by a repeat offender. Reynolds started Three Strikes and You're Out, an online resource, to provide the public with information on California's "three strikes" law. In the following report from the Web site, Reynolds maintains that California's "three strikes" law is an effective deterrent to career criminals and that the law is fair, cost-effective, and has resulted in a lower crime rate.

As you read, consider the following questions:

1. How much does the author say crime has dropped in California since the three-strikes law was passed?
2. How many new prisons have been built in California in the past 15 years, according to Reynolds?
3. What is California's prison population, according to the author?

"15 Years of 3 Strikes, 1994 to 2008, And Still Working!" Fresno, CA: Three Strikes, 2008. Reproduced by permission.

Most of those who believe in intervention have assigned some program that reinstates inner values, or has caused former offenders to reconsider the harm that their previous act had done, and what harm their current act will do.

Deterrents are the consideration an offender thinks over before re-offending. Considerations like: "Will I get caught?" "Will I be convicted?" "Will I actually go to jail or prison?" and . . . "If I do go to prison, for how long?"

Intervention vs. Deterrence

While intervention programs are seen as a "velvet glove" approach, the "Three Strikes" law is perceived as the "brass knuckles" technique, or deterrence.

The real question is . . . "What really works?"

Intervention and rehabilitation programs should be monitored and audited for effectiveness. These are very costly to taxpayers and we must have programs that have proven track records . . . or they need to be eliminated.

The California Department of Correction and Rehabilitation has been unable to provide accurate tracking of its inmates, due to an obsolete state computer system.

An Effective Deterrent

There are, however, three studies on California's "Three Strikes" offenders that show the likelihood of felons with one or two strikes having a dramatically less chance of returning with a new conviction than felons without prior "strike" convictions. These studies also show an extraordinary exodus from California of paroled felons. . . .

There is a clear and effective deterrence side to the "Three Strikes" law.

As to terminology of deterrence or intervention . . . if an offender has been deterred from committing a new crime, then you have intervened. The results are the same . . . and it is the results that count. For every offender that actually is sent to prison under "Three Strikes," countless others have given up a life of crime, or have left California.

Measuring Effectiveness

1. Does the condition improve after [the law's] passage?

2. Is it cost effective?

3. Is it fair?

These are simple rules to be guidelines for judging the success, or failure, of laws.

1. *Does the condition improve after its passage?*

The drop in overall crime that came after the passage of "Three Strikes" speaks for itself.

Historic drops in crime occurred within 3 years of the passage of "Three Strikes." We have since gone on to roll back crime rates to the 1968 era . . . "a 40-year reduction." The exception is residential burglary, which is at the same rate as 1953, a rate that hasn't been seen in over one-half a century. While there has been some modest rate changes—both up and down—the overall 15-year period, after "Three Strikes," has cut crime nearly in half. These are sustained crime reductions California has never previously experienced.

Anybody, with any level of objectivity, would have to believe "Three Strikes" is playing a major role in California's record crime reduction.

2. *Is it cost effective?*

Is letting criminals out of prison cheaper than keeping them in?

While there are those who argue great savings by releasing repeat offenders, one must consider, by definition, that a repeat offender is in and out of prison on a repetitive basis. The real question is: is there any savings by letting repeat offenders out for short amounts of time? Is the cost of catching and reconvicting them worth the small amount of time they are out? Do the crimes they commit while they are free outweigh the costs of incarceration?

Cost projections were that "Three Strikes" would add 20 new prisons and increase inmate populations to 250,000 in just 5 years. Financial estimates were over $4 billion per year. What was not understood is [that] when crime is cut in half that translates into not only fewer victims, but also fewer criminals that would have needed police investigations, court services for prosecution, and more prisons to house them.

Five years prior to "Three Strikes," California funded and built 19 new prisons. Only one new prison has been funded and built in the last 15 years, since "Three Strikes," and that is Delano 2. Today, California's prison population is 170,000. This represents only a 10,000 inmate growth in the last 9 years. Prior to "Three Strikes," prisons could see that much growth in a single year. Keep in mind, California saw its overall population increase by over 6.5 million people, since 1994, when the "Three Strikes" law was put into effect.

This represents an extraordinarily modest growth in prison population when considering such a large increase in new California residents. Everyone's attention is focused on California's 170,000 inmates. Few people know that nearly 125,000 are paroled each year.

Yes, California paroles nearly 125,000 inmates each year. 71% are back in and locked up within 18 months. The key to this equation is best seen in 3 million fewer victims and $54 billion dollars saved by reduced crime. This is a combination that saves lives and money.

3. *Is it fair?*

Are people getting life sentences for minor offenses?

There are 3 kinds of crimes: infractions, misdemeanors and felonies. The most serious of these are felonies. "Three Strikes" requires the first 2 convictions to be not just felonies, but serious or violent felonies, that are the "worst of the worst"

14 Year Differences

14 years before "Three Strikes" and 14 years after it became law

	Murders	Rape	Robberies	Assaults	Burglaries
Before	44,986	173,093	1,388,470	1,981,078	6,301,416
After	35,601	138,114	1,039,663	1,986,517	3,750,570
Difference	**9,385**	**34,979**	**348,807**	**−5,439**	**2,550,846**

TAKEN FROM: Threestrikes.org, 2008.

crimes. The third strike still requires a felony conviction in order to hand down a "25 to Life" sentence. Keep in mind, "Three Strikes" does not decide what is, or is not, a crime or what should be a serious or violent felony, or a misdemeanor. Our state legislature decides what crimes should be felonies, and what should be serious or violent felonies. In raising crime to the high threshold of a felony, be assured "minor" is not a part of a felony crime.

What is sometimes mistaken (or misunderstood) is the level of violence and brutality, as compared to the value of something rather minor. My daughter, Kimber, was murdered over a "minor" purse snatching. In fact, most murders are over little or "minor value" issues. Keep in mind, every "Three Strikes" case is closely reviewed by prosecutors who must prove the prior convictions in court. In the event that the defendant is found guilty of the current felony offense, the judge can, and does, review the merits of the case to decide whether or not to apply the full "25 to Life," or reduce the case to a second strike.

On average, only 1 out of every 9 eligible third strikers gets a "25 to Life" sentence.

The average third striker has 5 prior serious or violent felony convictions.

Are You Sure It's Three Strikes?

When you can't argue with the numbers (in this case, the reduction of crime after the passage of Three Strikes), then question the cause.

How do you know it's Three Strikes causing the reduction?

Criminologists have universally assigned crime trends to demographics that relate to population and the age groups contained within that population. Certain age groups have more frequent criminal behavior.

The other factor, that is often cited as a major influence, is the economy. A bad economy translates into fewer jobs and more of the unemployed turn to crime.

California's population expansion has been well documented in this study. This, over 50% increase in residents over the last 28 years, showcases every age bracket with larger populations, including those in the crime prone years. Yet crime is down.

Over the last 15 years of Three Strikes we have seen our economy go up and down, yet perhaps never as far down as it is today. Unemployment hits a new high every month. Using the economic model before us today, we should see runaway crime trends. With the exception of the "once in a while" front page act of violence, the actual number of crimes has held steady, and approximately one-half the rate prior to Three Strikes.

Poor education is also often referenced as a cause of crime. California's dropout rates have never been higher. With fewer students finishing high school we should find more of them turning to crime . . . but we're not.

Cause and Effect Difficult to Prove

A classic case in point is the association of cigarette smoke and lung cancer. It took over 40 years before conclusive proof was accepted, resulting in widespread public recognition of the definitive risk to smokers.

Another public health risk is crime. Crime is responsible for killing over 2,000 Californians every year. Many more are injured, maimed, and left in shattered shells of their former lives.

What is the cause of this crime?

If crime cannot be blamed on the poor economy, or an increase in population, or lack of education, then what can possibly be the cause of crime? Just maybe the leading cause of crime is "criminals."

Studies have shown that an extraordinarily high portion of our crime is committed by a rather small percentage of our criminals. They are by definition, "repeat offenders." This is exactly the targeted groups that Three Strikes has impacted—the smallest number of criminals that are responsible for the largest number of crimes.

In review: Possible causes that could be responsible for crime reduction.

1. Population is more, not less, thus it is eliminated.
2. The economy is down, yet so is crime.
3. Lack of education, higher dropout rates, but lower crime rates.

When you have eliminated everything but the obvious, then it is most likely the obvious—laws that are tougher on criminals "work." And Three Strikes has led the way.

VIEWPOINT 4

> *"If any sentence is grossly disproportionate, surely it is life imprisonment for shoplifting."*

California's "Three Strikes" Law Is Unfair

Erwin Chemerinsky

Erwin Chemerinsky is a constitutional law scholar and founding dean of the University of California at Irvine Law School. In the following viewpoint, he describes the case of Leandro Andrade, who was sentenced to life in prison for shoplifting $153 in children's videotapes from Kmart. Chemerinsky argues that Andrade's sentence is so harsh and unfair that it serves as a cogent reason for reforming California's "three strikes" law.

As you read, consider the following questions:

1. How did the Supreme Court vote on the Leandro Andrade appeal, as reported by Chemerinsky?
2. What did Justice David Souter say in his opinion on the case, according to the author?
3. According to Chemerinsky, how much does it cost to imprison a person for one year?

Erwin Chemerinsky, "3 Strikes: Cruel, Unusual and Unfair," *Los Angeles Times*, March 10, 2003, Opinion. Reproduced by permission of the author.

The U.S. Supreme Court's decisions upholding life imprisonment for shoplifters make reform of California's three-strikes law through the Legislature or the initiative process [i.e., by public referendum] imperative.

Today, 344 people are serving life sentences in California's prisons for shoplifting a small amount of merchandise. More than 650 individuals are serving life sentences for possessing small quantities of drugs. Such sentences make no rational sense and are inhumane.

Unfortunately, the high court's decisions mean that the only hope is for the Legislature to modify the three-strikes law to limit its application to those who commit serious or violent felonies. If the Legislature lacks the moral courage to make this simple change—and so far its members have been unwilling to do so—then there must be a voter initiative to revise the law.

The Case of Leandro Andrade

The Supreme Court, by a 5-4 vote, upheld the indeterminate life sentence with no possibility of parole for 50 years that Leandro Andrade received for stealing $153 worth of children's videotapes from Kmart.

An Army veteran and a father of three, Andrade never had committed a violent offense. He was 37 years old in 1996 when he was sentenced; his earliest possible parole date is 2046, when he will be 87 years old.

The other case the U.S. Supreme Court heard involved Gary Ewing, who received an indeterminate life sentence with no possibility of parole for 25 years for stealing three golf clubs.

For at least a century, the high court has held that grossly disproportionate sentences constitute cruel and unusual punishment in violation of the 8th Amendment. If any sentence is grossly disproportionate, surely it is life imprisonment for shoplifting.

Reforming California's Law

A meaningful discussion about California's criminal justice policy must include a reexamination of sentencing and the role of the courts. It must include a conversation about how to apply the right sentence to the right offender. It must address post-release supervision and the role of local communities in helping keep ex-offenders from backsliding. We must discuss increased latitude for judges and the curtailing of plea bargains. And any discussion must be bipartisan, with a focus on the science of criminal behavior—not on tough-on-crime bromides that are designed to scare the public.

Jeanne S. Woodford, Los Angeles Times, *August 6, 2006.*

Cruel and Unusual Punishment

As Justice David Souter observed in his dissenting opinion, "If Andrade's sentence is not grossly disproportionate, the principle has no meaning." In no other state could Andrade and Ewing have received these sentences. Every other state with a three-strikes law requires that the third strike be a serious or violent offense.

At the time Andrade and Ewing were convicted, the maximum penalty for rape was eight years in prison, for manslaughter, 11 years, and for second-degree murder, 15 years. Yet the U.S. Supreme Court says it is permissible to put shoplifters in prison for life.

Apart from being a cruel and unusual punishment, such a sentence for shoplifting makes no sense financially. It costs as much as $30,000 to imprison a person for a year. California is spending a large amount of money to incarcerate petty offenders—funds that could be better spent educating children or sheltering the homeless.

And many studies by social scientists have shown that the three-strikes law has no appreciable effect in decreasing crime.

An Unfair Law

The goal, though, is not to eliminate the three-strikes law. No one denies that repeat violent offenders should be imprisoned for long periods. Rather, the law must be changed so that it is not used to put people in prison for life for such offenses as shoplifting or possessing a small amount of drugs for personal use.

[In 2002], Assemblywoman Jackie Goldberg introduced a bill to modify the three-strikes law so that it could be used only for serious or violent offenders. Astoundingly, the day the legislation was introduced, Gov. Gray Davis announced that he would veto it. The bill did not pass.

Opinion polls show that the majority of Californians favor changing the law to require that the third strike be a serious or violent felony. But elected officials don't want to appear soft on crime, even when the crime is shoplifting. No politician wants to be vulnerable to a story of a shoplifter who was released and then committed a much worse crime.

Up to Legislators

Now that the U.S. Supreme Court has made clear that there will be no relief from inhumane sentences in the courts, legislators must show courage and change the law.

Otherwise, there must be an initiative in 2004 to revise the three-strikes law. Efforts are already underway to place an initiative on the ballot, but reform through the initiative process will be difficult.

Initiatives succeed best when they are well financed, and there is no wealthy constituency for reforming the three-strikes law.

A Travesty of Justice

I represented Leandro Andrade in the federal appeals court and the U.S. Supreme Court. Like so many people sentenced under the three-strikes law, he had committed a series of property crimes because of drug addiction.

Andrade already has served seven years in prison for stealing merchandise worth $153. He has 43 years left on his sentence and no hope from any court in the country.

In a nation that prides itself on basic human decency, and with a Constitution that prohibits cruel and unusual punishment, this just can't be right.

Viewpoint 5

> *"We have a moment in time that must be seized in order to ensure that all of our citizens are treated in a way that is consistent with the ideals embodied in our founding documents."*

Mandatory Minimum Sentences for Crack Cocaine Possession Are Unfair

Eric Holder

Eric Holder is the attorney general of the United States. In the following speech to commemorate the twenty-fifth anniversary of the Sentencing Reform Act of 1984, he reflects on the successes and failures of mandatory minimum sentencing. In particular, Holder asserts that the federal crack cocaine sentencing policy must undergo a rigorous review, because "the disparity in crack and powder cocaine sentences is unwarranted, creates a perception of unfairness, and must be eliminated."

As you read, consider the following questions:

1. According to Holder, how much has the U.S. prison population grown since 1980?

Eric Holder, "Rethinking Federal Sentencing Policy: 25th Anniversary of the Sentencing Reform Act," speech for the Charles Hamilton Houston Institute for Race and Justice and Congressional Black Caucus Symposium in Washington, D.C., June 24, 2009.

2. Why does the author believe that a perception of unfairness affects the criminal justice authority?
3. How does Holder describe the ideal sentencing scheme?

The federal sentencing system, which includes both sentencing guidelines and mandatory minimum sentencing statutes, has undergone significant change since the Supreme Court's decision in *United States v. Booker*. The guidelines continue to provide a sentencing baseline in all federal criminal cases. However, Sentencing Commission data show that the percentage of defendants sentenced within the guidelines has decreased since the decision. Although the full impact of recent trends in sentencing jurisprudence is still unclear, these developments should be monitored carefully. For example, we should assess whether current sentencing practices show an increase in unwarranted sentencing disparities based upon regional differences or even differences in judicial philosophy among judges working in the same courthouse. But we must also be prepared to accept the fact that not every disparity is an unwelcome one. The desire to have an almost mechanical system of sentencing has led us away from individualized, fact-based determinations that I believe, within reason, should be our goal.

We must also be aware of the fact that the federal inmate population continues to increase. This development puts an enormous strain on correctional resources. The number of inmates in federal prisons, state prisons, or local jails has quadrupled since 1980, reaching more than 2.2 million today. Of particular concern, the burgeoning prison population limits the ability of corrections officials to provide drug treatment and other services necessary to minimize recidivism [relapse into crime]. A 2002 study from the Bureau of Justice Statistics tracked a sample of more than a quarter-million prisoners released in 15 states in 1994. Within three years, two-thirds of these offenders were rearrested at least once for a new offense,

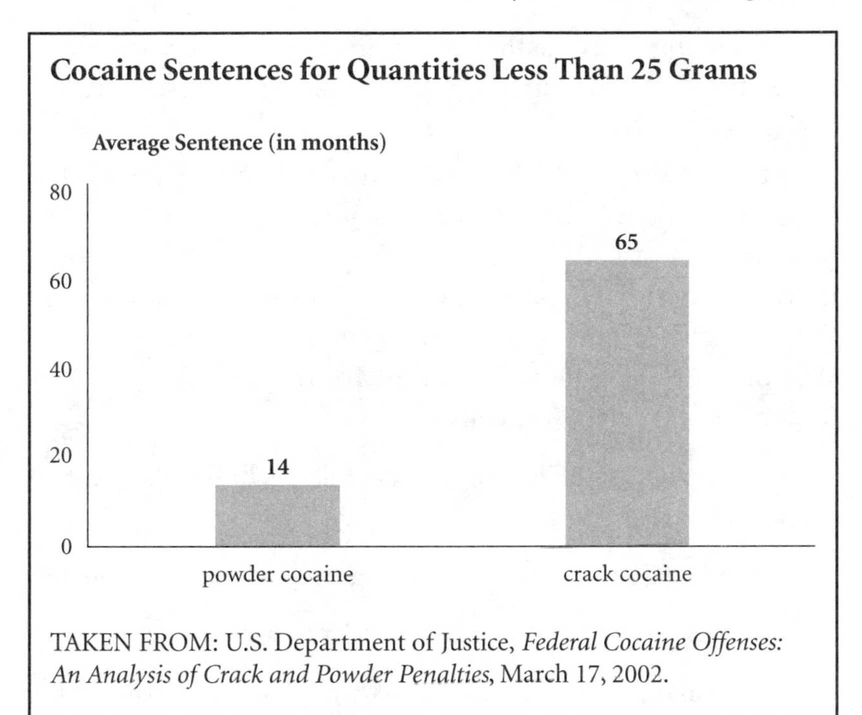

TAKEN FROM: U.S. Department of Justice, *Federal Cocaine Offenses: An Analysis of Crack and Powder Penalties*, March 17, 2002.

nearly half were convicted for a new crime, and another quarter were re-sentenced to prison for a new conviction.

A Review Is Necessary

The current federal sentencing system continues to be a target for criticism from judges, academics, and attorneys across our nation. These criticisms range from concerns about mandatory minimums to the use of acquitted conduct in sentencing decisions. Accordingly, a thorough review of federal sentencing and corrections policies, with an eye toward possible reform, is welcome and necessary.

The twenty-fifth anniversary of the Sentencing Reform Act provides a good opportunity to reflect on the state of federal sentencing. The U.S. Sentencing Commission has begun a review of the impact of *Booker* and of the federal sentencing system as a whole by soliciting testimony at regional hearings.

Those hearings will identify those practices that contribute to the goals of the Sentencing Reform Act, and those practices that do not.

At the same time, the Department of Justice [DOJ] has begun its own internal review of sentencing and corrections policy. I have asked members of the DOJ community—both in Washington, DC and in the U.S. Attorneys Offices around the country—to participate in the Sentencing and Corrections Working Group which is chaired by the Deputy Attorney General. Our review will consider:

- the structure of federal sentencing, including the role of mandatory minimums;
- the Department's own charging and sentencing policies;
- alternatives to incarceration and re-entry;
- eliminating the sentencing disparity between crack and powder cocaine; and
- an examination of other unwarranted disparities in federal sentencing.

As part of that review, we are soliciting the input of key stakeholders such as law enforcement, members of Congress, the defense and advocacy community, and judges.

Set of Core Values

We are approaching this effort with a specific set of core values. We will apply those principles to create a sentencing and corrections system that protects the public, is fair to both victims and defendants, eliminates unwarranted sentencing disparities, reduces recidivism, and controls the federal prison population. In doing so we must create a system that allows us to dismantle gangs and drug trafficking organizations that plague too many of our nation's streets, and that allows us to effectively combat offenses as varied as violent crime, child exploitation, sex trafficking, and financial fraud. But focusing on punishment is not enough. The federal sentencing system must also embrace the President's commitment to reducing recidivism and providing opportunities to offenders to become contributing members of society at the conclusion of their sentence.

Public trust and confidence are also essential elements of an effective criminal justice system. Our laws and their enforcement must not only be fair, they also must be perceived as fair. A perception of unfairness undermines governmental authority in the criminal justice process. It leads victims and witnesses of crime to think twice before cooperating with law enforcement, tempts jurors to ignore the law and facts when deciding a criminal case, and causes the public to question the motives of government officials. Accordingly, we must create a system where the factual basis for sentencing in a particular case is clear to all parties and to the public, and where the sentences themselves are truly commensurate with the crime committed.

Crack Cocaine Disparity

One thing is very clear to me: we must review our federal cocaine sentencing policy. Fifteen years ago, the United States Sentencing Commission first reported on the differences in sentencing between crack and powder cocaine. Since then, the need to reassess the federal cocaine sentencing laws has only grown stronger. This Administration firmly believes that the disparity in crack and powder cocaine sentences is unwarranted, creates a perception of unfairness, and must be eliminated. This change should be addressed in Congress.

Many of you in Congress already have introduced or cosponsored legislation to address the disparity between crack and powder cocaine. We look forward to working with you and other Members of Congress over the coming months to deal with this issue.

There is no tension between a sentencing scheme that is effective and fair and one that is tough and equitable. We must work toward these twin goals and we must do so now. Too much time has passed, too many people have been treated in a disparate manner, and too many of our citizens have come to have doubts about our criminal justice system. We must be honest with each other and have the courage to ask difficult questions of ourselves and our system. We must break out of the old and tired partisan stances that have stood in the way of needed progress and reform. We have a moment in time that must be seized in order to ensure that all of our citizens are treated in a way that is consistent with the ideals embodied in our founding documents.

> *"Current federal cocaine sentencing policy is properly calibrated and advances the law enforcement response to crack cocaine in a fair and just manner."*

Mandatory Minimum Sentences for Crack Cocaine Possession Are Fair

R. Alexander Acosta

R. Alexander Acosta is the U.S. attorney in the Southern District of Florida. In the following testimony during a U.S. Sentencing Commission hearing on federal cocaine sentencing policy, he argues that "federal drug sentencing policy is sound and fosters a fair and aggressive law enforcement response to the national drug problem." Acosta maintains that crack cocaine is more addictive, more potent, and more harmful and results in more violence and societal harm than does powder cocaine, which, he contends, justifies the higher penalties for crack cocaine offenses.

As you read, consider the following questions:

1. What societal harms flow from the use and distribution of crack, according to the author?

R. Alexander Acosta, "Federal Cocaine Sentencing Policy," Testimony of the U.S. Department of Justice Before the U.S. Sentencing Commission, November 14, 2006.

2. According to Acosta, what is the basic structure of drug trafficking organizations?
3. What does the author describe as the three broad levels of crack trafficking?

As the [U.S. Sentencing] Commission knows, sentencing policy for drug offenses is a critical component of the effort to disrupt and dismantle drug trafficking organizations. It would be of little value to investigate and break up a violent drug gang, only to see the members of that gang return to the community in short order to continue their work. In 1987, working in a coordinated fashion with Congress and the Executive Branch, the Sentencing Commission tied the sentencing guidelines and federal drug penalties for drug trafficking offenses to the type and quantity of drug associated with the offense. These guidelines, found at §2D1.1 of the sentencing guidelines, call for base offense levels ranging from level 6 to level 38, moving in two-level increments determined by the type and quantity of drugs trafficked by the defendant.

Current Sentencing Guidelines

The guidelines are tied—by law—to the applicable mandatory minimum drug trafficking statutes passed by Congress. The amount of controlled substance that triggers a mandatory minimum corresponds to a base offense level calibrated with the mandatory penalty. For example, five grams of actual methamphetamine triggers a mandatory minimum sentence of five years and is tied to a base offense level of 26 with a corresponding sentence of 63–78 months under the guidelines for a first offender. Title 21 U.S.C. § 841 specifies the quantity thresholds that trigger mandatory minimum sentences. Some observers have criticized the present sentencing guidelines scheme, arguing that this quantity-based scheme does not adequately address other relevant sentencing factors. We disagree.

Current law—both in the federal statutes and the guidelines—allows for appropriate consideration of aggravating factors such as the use of a gun or a defendant's criminal history or bodily injury. Current law also allows for the consideration of mitigating factors, through the "safety valve" exception to mandatory minimums, the guidelines' mitigating role adjustment and mitigating role cap, the acceptance of responsibility adjustment, and guideline departures when a defendant provides substantial assistance in the investigation or prosecution of another person.

Overall, we believe the structure of federal drug sentencing policy is sound and fosters a fair and aggressive law enforcement response to the national drug problem.

Cocaine Sentencing Policy

We similarly believe the current federal cocaine sentencing policy is properly calibrated and advances the law enforcement response to crack cocaine in a fair and just manner. We continue to believe higher penalties for crack cocaine offenses appropriately reflect the greater harm posed by crack cocaine; harms recognized by the Commission consistently since 1995. While cocaine base—crack—and cocaine hydrochloride—cocaine powder—are chemically similar, there are significant differences in the predominant way the two substances are ingested and marketed. Based on these differences and the resulting harms to society, crack cocaine is an especially dangerous drug, and its traffickers should be subject to significantly higher penalties than traffickers of like amounts of cocaine powder. We will address these differences in turn.

Crack More Potent and Addictive

An examination of the pharmacology and most common routes of administration of powder and crack cocaine reveals that crack is more potent and addictive, resulting in more emergency-room episodes and public-facility treatment admissions than powder cocaine, despite the fact that powder cocaine is much more widely used. The quicker, more intense, and shorter-duration effects of smoked crack contribute to its greater abuse and dependency potential as compared to snorted cocaine powder. Its greater addictive effects cause heavier and more frequent use and greater binging, causing more severe social and behavioral changes than use of cocaine powder.

The highest concentration of cocaine and the fastest entry to the central nervous system occur when cocaine is smoked. Smoking is one of the most efficient ways to take a psychoactive drug. The amount of cocaine that is absorbed through the large surface area of the lungs by smoking is greater even than the amount absorbed by injecting a solution of cocaine. In addition, the ease of smoking allows a user to ingest extreme levels of the drug in the body without repeatedly filling a syringe, finding injection sites, and then actually injecting oneself. The intensity of the euphoria, the speed with which it is attained, and the ease of repeat administration are factors that explain the user attraction to crack.

Differences in distribution methods, age groups involved, and levels of violence between crack and powder—all discussed more ahead—flow from the fact that smaller amounts of crack are needed to produce the euphoria that is sought by the typical user. Crack can be distributed in smaller unit sizes than powder cocaine and is sold in single dose units at prices that are at first easily affordable by the young and the poor. Because crack is distributed in such relatively small amounts in transactions that often occur on street corners, control of small geographic areas by traffickers takes on great importance. As a result, crack offenders are more likely to possess a weapon, and crack is often associated with serious crime related to its marketing and distribution, especially violent street crime connected with gangs, guns, serious injury and death. The struggle to gain and maintain that geographic control is infused with great violence. All of this flows from the pharmacology of crack.

Other Societal Harms

Moreover, other societal harms flow from the ease of use and distribution of crack. In a study of drug use and societal harms, fully one-third of crack-using women surveyed became involved in prostitution in the year after they began crack use. Women who were already involved in prostitution dramatically increased their involvement, with rates nearly four times higher than before beginning crack use. Because of the incidence of prostitution among crack users to finance their habit, crack cocaine smokers have been found to have rates of HIV infection as high as those among IV [intravenous] drug users.

Similarly, a 2001 study found that women who used crack cocaine had "much higher than average rates of victimization" than women who did not, and were more likely to be attacked and more likely to be raped. Although the study did not compare the victimization rates with other drug-using groups, it nevertheless starkly reflected the tremendous human toll this drug takes. Among an Ohio sample of 171 non-drug-injecting adult female crack users, 62% had been physically attacked from the onset of crack use. Rape was reported by 32% of the women from the time they began using crack, and among these, 83% reported being high on crack when the rape occurred, as were an estimated 57% of the perpetrators.

Cocaine Trafficking Patterns

Cocaine trafficking patterns, moreover, lead to high rates of violence associated with both powder and crack cocaine trafficking, but especially with crack trafficking.

As noted above, it is important to recognize that crack cocaine does not typically enter the distribution chain in the chemical form that makes it crack cocaine; rather, it enters the distribution chain as powder cocaine, and at some point later in the distribution chain, is converted into the form known as crack. For this reason, the Administration recognizes that disrupting the cocaine market at its highest levels will have benefits in addressing both powder cocaine and the crack cocaine trafficking domestically.

At the highest levels, powder cocaine is generally trafficked in metric-ton quantities by sophisticated criminal enterprises that manage its shipment from source countries to major markets in the United States. The Drug Trafficking Organizations ("DTOs") of today maintain an infrastructure of compartmentalized cells, each managed by a cell head and having a specific function in the overall scheme of the DTO's illicit drug trade. The Colombian DTOs are still controlled by a hierarchy; however, these current leaders are content to detach themselves from outgoing loads of illicit drugs once handed off to an entirely separate organization, typically in Mexico. The Colombian DTOs of today may be described as a loose confederation, coexisting and cooperating with each other, while aided and supported by guerilla and paramilitary groups indigenous to Colombia.

Journey of Illicit Drugs

Transportation of illicit drugs within the interior of Colombia is accomplished only with the assistance of these paramilitary and guerilla groups, who complete the task through the use of both riverboats, in Colombia's dense jungles, and containerized loads hauled by tractor trailers over paved regions of the country. The illicit drugs are ultimately brought to Colombia's north and west coasts where they then leave the country through maritime smuggling operations, specifically through the use of go-fast boats. Once the illicit drugs arrive in Mexico or Central America, the Mexican DTOs take custody and the drugs are transported through Mexico in compartmentalized containers hauled by tractor trailer and most often concealed with perishables. The loads of illicit drugs are broken up into smaller parcels just prior to being smuggled into the United States. This reduction in parcel size is typically accomplished at residences, purchased by the Mexican DTOs, within close proximity to the United States border.

Upon entry into the United States, the distribution of illicit drugs by the Mexican and Colombian DTOs is further compartmentalized, with the Mexican DTOs controlling the west coast of the United States and Colombian DTOs controlling the east coast of the United States, at the wholesale distribution level. The ultimate domestic destination of a shipment of illicit drugs is decided by the Colombian or Mexican DTO head. At times, the DTO's cell head within the United States influences this decision as well. Typically, once in the United States, final destination is based on the geographic lines set forth above. Security for the illicit drugs that have arrived in the United States is often provided by heavily armed members of the DTO. Upon completion of division into smaller parcels, the illicit drugs are then turned over to the buyer or member of the DTO operating in the United States. The illicit drugs are then transported to the domestic cities predetermined by the DTO for ultimate retail sale.

At this point, the cocaine shipment is generally divided into even smaller amounts for sale to local wholesalers, who distribute 15-kilogram or fewer quantities. The local wholesalers sell kilogram amounts to retail distribution groups that further divide the cocaine for retail sales. Retail distribution groups repackage cocaine purchases in ounce and gram quantities for sale by that group or other smaller retailers. While there continues to be a market for powder cocaine at the retail level, primarily among casual users and cocaine injectors, crack distribution and abuse now constitute an important force behind the current cocaine threat in the United States.

Crack Distribution Methods

Although crack trafficking methods vary widely, generally, they are conducted at three broad levels, namely, wholesale trafficking, mid-level distribution, and retail selling. Wholesale crack traffickers purchase cocaine in kilogram or multi-kilogram allotments from traditional cocaine sources. They will either package the cocaine into ounce quantities or convert it into crack and then divide it into ounces for sale at the next level. Wholesalers represent large groups responsible for the majority of the interstate transportation of crack and cocaine intended for crack conversion. Crack distributors further divide the ounces of crack into dosage units for sale at the retail level. If the distributors purchase cocaine themselves, they can perform the conversion process easily. These distributors often operate crack houses or manage street-corner sales locations and supervise up to 20 individual sellers. Mid-level distributors can be either members of larger groups or independent operators. Retail crack sellers carry dosage units of crack totaling no more than a few grams at any one time, although during the course of a work shift, the amount of crack sold by one retail seller can be substantial. Workers in crack houses will sell dosage units from the one or two ounces that are delivered by the mid-level distributors.

Crack cocaine is packaged in vials, glassine bags, film canisters, etc. Rock sizes are not precise, but they generally range from 1/10 to 1/2 gram. A retail or street dosage unit for crack is approximately 100 milligrams. These rocks can sell for as little as $2 to as much as $50. As Professor Randall Kennedy noted, "[b]ecause it is relatively inexpensive," crack has the "dubious 'achievement'" that it has "helped tremendously to democratize cocaine use." Crack is easier to package, transport and conceal than powder. Crack cocaine is not water soluble and can be more easily concealed in a piece of tissue, in the mouth, or in body cavities, allowing easier and wider distribution.

Crack generally is converted locally from cocaine and sold at the retail level. When crack is available in kilogram quantities, prices are comparable to those for kilogram quantities of cocaine, with modest price increases to compensate for the

What Is Cocaine?

Cocaine is a powerfully addictive stimulant that directly affects the brain. Cocaine is not a new drug. In fact, it is one of the oldest known drugs. The pure chemical, cocaine hydrochloride, has been an abused substance for more than 100 years, and coca leaves, the source of cocaine, have been ingested for thousands of years. . . .

Cocaine abuse has a long history and is rooted into the drug culture in the U.S. It is an intense euphoric drug with strong addictive potential. With the increase in purity, the advent of the free-base form of the cocaine ("crack"), and its easy availability on the street, cocaine continues to burden both the law enforcement and health care systems in America.

The powdered, hydrochloride salt form of cocaine can be snorted or dissolved in water and injected. Crack is cocaine that has not been neutralized by an acid to make the hydrochloride salt. This form of cocaine comes in a rock crystal that can be heated and its vapors smoked. The term "crack" refers to the crackling sound heard when it is heated.

U.S. Drug Enforcement Administration, 2009.

task of converting the cocaine into crack. The national range for prices of ounce quantities is from $475 to $2,800. A gram of crack generally costs between $80 and $125.

Cocaine Trafficking and Violence

Sentencing Commission data and other studies continue to show that crack cocaine is associated with violence to a greater degree than most other controlled substances. In fiscal year 2002, when the Administration last testified before the Commission on this subject, 23.1 percent of all federal crack offenders possessed a weapon, almost double that of powder cocaine's then 12.1 percent rate. In fiscal year 2005, weapon involvement for crack cocaine offenders was 27.8 percent versus 13.6 percent for powder cocaine offenders. In addition, the percentage of crack defendants at criminal history category VI—those offenders with long criminal records—increased to 23.5 percent in FY [fiscal year] 2005 from the 20.2 percent figure in FY 2002. A much smaller percentage of cocaine powder defendants were involved with a weapon or were at criminal history category VI in both 2002 and 2005.

Much of the crack cocaine violence is associated with gang activity, and drug gang violence has increased in recent years. Many drug gangs that traffic in crack cocaine include very young members who carry and use guns to promote their drug trafficking. Crack cocaine is associated more with street level gang violence than is cocaine powder, although gangs also deal in methamphetamine, PCP, and many other controlled substances. According to the 2005 National Gang Threat Assessment, 38 percent of law enforcement respondents reported moderate to high involvement of gangs in the distribution of powder cocaine, while 47.3 percent reported moderate to high involvement of gangs in the distribution of crack cocaine. National Drug Threat Assessment ("NDTS") 2004 data also show that gangs are very substantially involved in crack distribution, particularly in metropolitan areas. In fact, NDTS 2004 data indicate that 52.7 percent of state and local law enforcement agencies in large cities report high or moderate involvement of street gangs in crack distribution compared with 28.3 percent of state and local agencies in all areas.

Moreover, the National Institute of Justice's Arrestee Drug Abuse Monitoring ("ADAM") program 2000 urinalysis findings revealed that high percentages of ADAM arrestees had recently used cocaine—on average, 30 percent of arrestees tested

say so every five years. That the law has yet to be repealed is a testament to the persistence of age-old fallacies regarding race and class.

While drug use rates are similar among all racial groups, African American drug offenders have a 20 percent greater chance of being sentenced to prison than white offenders, according to Commission statistics. In 2005, more than 80 percent of crack cocaine defendants were black.

Meanwhile, President [George W.] Bush's recent commutation of Lewis 'Scooter' Libby's "excessive" 30-month prison sentence for outing a CIA agent has only added insult to injury.

"If President Bush truly believes that the power of commutation is necessary to correct injustice, there is no shortage of cases of people languishing in federal prisons for unconscionably lengthy sentences who are deserving of such attention," says Marc Mauer, executive director of The Sentencing Project, a Washington-based advocacy group.

Mauer's group—along with others such as Families Against Mandatory Minimums (FAMM) and the Drug Policy Alliance (DPA)—is part of a vocal coalition aimed at pressuring lawmakers to take action to reform the law. Mauer recently testified before a House subcommittee hearing on mandatory minimums, telling Congress that mandatory penalties for crack cocaine "inevitably result in disproportionate prosecutions of low-level offenders, precisely the opposite of what federal policy should encourage."

At its core, the crack law is a glaring example of the bad policy decisions that often follow a national tragedy—in this case the overdose death of University of Maryland basketball star Len Bias. Within months of Bias' death in June 1986, Congress pushed through the law with overwhelming support from both parties, and in 1988 extended the mandatory penalty to include simple possession of crack.

Recent Attempts at Reform

In May 2007, the USSC [U.S. Sentencing Commission] issued a report imploring Congress to act quickly to eliminate the sentencing disparity between crack and powder cocaine. Although federal law still calls for mandatory minimums triggered by the net weight of illicit substance, the USSC has now amended their sentencing guidelines, and applied the change retroactively, to lessen the punishment range for crack cocaine cases by approximately one to two years. The Commission's changes will reduce the average sentence from a little more than 10 years to a little under 9 years and will affect thousands of defendants in our criminal justice system.

In December 2007, the U.S. Sentencing Commission voted to make the amendment retroactive. The practical effect of that vote is to make up to 19,500 currently incarcerated individuals eligible for early release over 30 years, after judicial review in each case.

Drug Policy Alliance, 2007.

"Congress was responding to a media and political frenzy and passed the law in record time, really, without any input from experts or drug abuse specialists to determine what the appropriate response might be," explains Mauer. "It was a very narrow approach that failed to take into account the broad subject of substance abuse."

While it was eventually revealed that Bias actually died of a powder cocaine overdose, the racist notion that as a young black man he must have been smoking crack persisted in the media. That misinformation, coupled with the mounting hysteria surrounding the recently launched "War on Drugs," lent credence to a new zero-tolerance movement.

The long-term ramifications of the law soon became obvious. Over the past two decades jails and prisons across the country have been filled to capacity with low-level dealers and users, while suppliers continue to evade justice. According to data from The Sentencing Project, a sampling of those incarcerated under the guidelines in 2000 showed roughly 66 percent were low-level street dealers, while only half-of-one percent qualified as "high-level" suppliers.

Subsequently, an entire generation of young, poor, mostly black men is spending large chunks of time behind bars, some for no more a crime than holding a few rocks.

"The effect has been significant," says Mauer. "The Sentencing Commission has laid out in clear terms that this policy was a failure; that it isn't an effective way of addressing the problem of drug addiction—that is, it just isn't working—and because of the obvious racial disparity that was built into it."

The racial component of the law is especially troubling. The Bureau of Justice Statistics found that between 1994 and 2003, the average time African American drug offenders served in prison increased by 77 percent, compared to an increase of 28 percent for white drug offenders. As a result, African Americans now serve, on average, virtually as much time in jail for drug offenses as whites do for violent crimes.

"The policy of the federal government is having a devastating effect on our communities and that these laws continue to be maintained show, at the very least, a callous disregard for our people and our communities," said Hilary Shelton, director of the NAACP's [National Association for the Advancement of Colored People] Washington Bureau, testifying before the Sentencing Commission in November. "It is this disregard for the fate of our people and our community that continues to erode our confidence in our nation's criminal justice system."

[In 2007], as it has four times in the past two decades, the Commission recommended that lawmakers repeal the crack sentencing mandate. In a 202-page report released on May 15, the Commission maintained its consistently held position that the 100-to-1 drug quantity ratio significantly undermines the various congressional objectives set forth in the Sentencing Reform Act and urged Congress to take legislative action to reform the system.

Some lawmakers appear to have finally taken that message to heart.

"I think increasingly there's been a bipartisan movement for some kind of reform," says Mauer. "Back in 2002, Senators Jeff Sessions and Orrin Hatch introduced a sort of compromise proposal that would have raised the threshold for crack while lowering the threshold for powder. That was significant because it was coming from two leading conservatives. That was a turning point of sorts; I think since then both in the House and Senate there's been more support for change." . . .

Mauer says it's encouraging that legislators are finally addressing what he calls the "unconscionable racial disparities" inherent in the federal crack sentencing guidelines; but he insists it's only a first step.

"This is by far the most significant pace of reform we've seen in some time," says Mauer of the legislation currently in process. "Under the circumstances, I think equalization is the only defensible alternative, but even then they impose a mandatory sentence, which we think is fundamentally flawed. Crack is just part of the broader issue of mandatory minimums, and it's typical of what's wrong with this system."

> *"Decreasing the average time served for crack cocaine offenses . . . would harm the overall effort to keep drugs off the street and violence out of our communities."*

Mandatory Minimum Sentences for Crack Cocaine Possession Should Not Be Decreased

Chuck Canterbury

Chuck Canterbury is the national president of the Fraternal Order of Police (FOP). In the following viewpoint, he articulates FOP's opposition to dealing with the crack-powder cocaine disparity by decreasing the penalty for crack cocaine offenses. Canterbury stresses the dangers of crack cocaine—particularly the damage it inflicts on individuals and communities—and proposes that if Congress wants to eliminate the crack-powder cocaine disparity, it should increase penalties for powder cocaine offenses.

Chuck Canterbury, "Federal Cocaine Sentencing Policy," Testimony at a Public Hearing Before U.S. Sentencing Commission, November 14, 2006. Reproduced by permission of the author.

As you read, consider the following questions:

1. According to Canterbury, what total percentage of cocaine users admitted to hospital in 2005 were crack cocaine users?
2. What is the specific FOP proposal to decrease the crack-powder disparity, according to the author?
3. How many Americans does the National Institute on Drug Abuse, as cited here, estimate used cocaine in 2007?

Drug abuse and narcotics trafficking in the United States has always been a top concern of our nation's law enforcement agencies. But in the 1980s, our nation experienced an explosion in violence that was fueled almost entirely by the emergence of crack cocaine—a cheaper, more dangerous form of the drug, which was revealed to have a devastating psychological and physiological effect on its users. The rapid spread of crack cocaine's use and availability in our nation's major cities caught many of us in the law enforcement community by surprise, particularly the increased number of related crimes and the violence on the part of drug dealers trying to protect their turf and users who were willing to do anything to pay for their next fix. As a result, drug-related crime became our nation's number-one source of crime and law enforcement's number-one priority.

Congress moved quickly to confront this violence and the ongoing threat of crime and addiction by giving law enforcement the tools they needed to combat drug traffickers and dealers. Measures like the Anti-Drug Abuse Acts of 1986 and 1988 put stiffer penalties into place for those who would bring the poison of drugs and violence into our neighborhoods and communities. In the experience of the FOP, tougher penalties work. They worked in the 1980s and 1990s and were a very significant factor in the ability of law enforcement to counter the "crack" explosion. Mandatory minimum sentences, especially those which take into consideration the type of drug, the presence or use of firearms, the use or attempted use of violence, mean longer sentences for the worst offenders. The lessons law enforcement learned in fighting the "crack wars" of the 1980s have been applied to other anti-narcotic and anti-crime strategies and have proven to be effective. As recently as [2006], Congress adopted the Combat Meth Act which provides enhanced sentences for persons smuggling methamphetamines or the precursor chemicals needed to manufacture this drug into the United States, for persons who function as meth "kingpins" and for those who manufacture or deal the drug where children live or are present. According to local and state law enforcement, the abuse and manufacture of methamphetamines is the number-one law enforcement problem in the nation and Congress has acted to give us the tools we need to bring this problem under control by using the success we had in fighting crack as a model.

The Crack Cocaine Disparity

The current sentencing guidelines for cocaine offenses are based primarily on the quantity of the drug in the possession of the defendant at the time of his arrest and the law does make a significant distinction between the possession of crack and cocaine in its powder form. Under current guidelines, a person convicted of distributing 500 grams of powder cocaine or 5 grams of crack cocaine receives a mandatory 5-year sentence, and a 10-year sentence for those convicted of distributing 5,000 grams of powder or 50 grams of crack. This Commission and Congress has considered the impact of this disparity on several occasions. In a report to Congress in 1997 required by Public Law 104-38, this Commission recognized that some drugs "have more attendant harms than others and that those who traffic in more dangerous drugs ought to be sentenced more severely than those who traffic in less dangerous drugs." The FOP believe that the evidence demonstrates that crack cocaine does in fact inflict greater harm to both the user and to environment—the communities—in which it is available. One such example is that while only 22% of all cocaine users use crack cocaine, they represented 72% of all primary admissions to hospitals for cocaine usage in [2005].

The Commission's findings in the 1997 report also stated that crack cocaine is more often associated with systemic crime, is more widely available on the street, is particularly accessible to the most vulnerable members of our society, and produces more intense physiological and psychotropic effects than the use of powder cocaine. As a result, Federal sentencing policy must reflect the greater dangers associated with crack and impose correspondingly greater punishments. The FOP agrees strongly with this assessment. Anyone who has ever seen a child or adult addicted to crack, or talked to the families who are forced to live locked inside their own homes for fear of the crack dealers who rule their streets, would also agree with this statement.

Mitigating Factors to Consider

There are, however, other factors which should go into the sentencing of those convicted of crack-powder cocaine offenses. The Commission notes that some have suggested that proportionality in drug sentences could be better served by providing enhancements that target offenders who engage in aggravating conduct, and by reducing the penalties based solely on the quantity of crack cocaine to the extent that the Drug Quantity Table already takes aggravating conduct into account. For example, possession of 5 grams of crack is currently assigned a base offense level of 26, which translates into a sentence of between 63 and 78 months for individuals with 0 to 1 Criminal History Points. The Commission has previously considered a differentiation regarding the use and possession of firearms in drug-related offenses, and providing

National Survey on Drug Use and Health

According to the 2007 National Survey on Drug Use and Health, 35.9 million Americans aged 12 and older reported having used cocaine, and 8.6 million reported having used crack. An estimated 2.1 million Americans were current (past-month) users of cocaine; 610,000 were current users of crack. There were an estimated 906,000 new users of cocaine in 2007—most were 18 or older when they first used cocaine. Among young adults aged 18 to 25, the past-year use rate was 6.4 percent, showing no significant difference from the previous year.

National Institute on Drug Abuse, June 2009.

sentencing enhancements for the distribution of drugs at a protected location or to underage or pregnant individuals. We believe that the sentencing guidelines should include additional aggravating factors—the presence of firearms or children, use or attempted use of violence are a few examples—in the determination of a final sentence. However, these and other enhancements should continue to be in addition to a reasonable mandatory minimum sentence that is based first and foremost on the quantity of the controlled substance as provided for under current law.

The FOP has heard and appreciates the concerns of some regarding the 100:1 drug quantity ratio for crack cocaine and powder cocaine offenses. As I mentioned previously, we testified before this Commission on that very issue several years ago and we continue to reject proposals which would "fix" this disparity by *decreasing* the penalties which have proven to be effective in law enforcement's fight against crack cocaine.

We hold that this approach is at variance with common sense and strongly disagree with the assumption that 5- and 10-year mandatory sentences should be targeted only at the most serious drug offenders. The so-called "low level dealer," who traffics in small amounts of either powder or crack cocaine, is no less of a danger to the community than an individual at the manufacturing or wholesale level. Despite the fact that these individuals may represent the bottom of the drug distribution chain does not necessarily translate into a decrease in the risk of violence that all too often accompanies these offenses, or in the serious threat they pose to the safety of our children and the quality of life in our communities. A 2002 report published by this Commission stated that "the majority of crack cocaine and powder cocaine offenders performed low-level trafficking functions" and that "aggravating factors occurred more often in crack cocaine cases than in powder cocaine cases." The most recent report from the Arrestee Drug Abuse Monitoring (ADAM) Program indicates that in four major metropolitan areas (Miami, Phoenix, Seattle, and Tucson), the number of transactions in the crack market was much larger than in the powder cocaine and marijuana markets. In these sites, the estimated size (measured in dollars) of the crack cocaine market in a 30-day period was 2 to 10 times larger than the size of the powder cocaine and marijuana markets. The range among these sites in the market size of crack cocaine was about $226,000 to $1,400,000.

Crack and Powder Are Different

Powder cocaine, while the same in some respects to crack cocaine, does not have the same impact on a community, nor is it associated with the same type of related crime. The efforts of law enforcement to control it must be different as well. The Fraternal Order of Police would support *increasing* the penalties for offenses involving powder cocaine through a reduction in the quantity of powder necessary to trigger the 5- and 10-

year mandatory minimum sentences, thereby decreasing the gap between the two similar offenses and addressing the concerns of those who question the current ratio without depriving law enforcement with the tools they need to control the possession, use, and sale of powder cocaine.

There are other reasons to support an increase in the penalties associated with cocaine-related offenses. In its 1995 report on "Cocaine and Federal Sentencing Policy," the Commission wrote that the Drug Enforcement Administration noted that in prior years some wholesale distributors who initially handled crack cocaine were moving to distribute powder cocaine to avoid the "harsh Federal sentencing guidelines that apply to higher-volume crack sales." More recently, in its 2002 edition, the Commission noted that while average prison sentence for someone convicted of possessing crack cocaine has remained fairly static from 1992 to 2000 (an average of 118 months), the average prison sentence for someone found violating the powder cocaine statutes has decreased from 99 months in prison to 74 months in prison—that is 40 percent less than those convicted of possession of crack cocaine. The FOP would strongly oppose attempts to equalize the outcome by decreasing the average time served for crack cocaine offenses, as we believe such an approach would harm the overall effort to keep drugs off the street and violence out of our communities. . . .

The Fraternal Order of Police supports tough penalties for all drug-related offenses. Each illegal drug carries with it different effects on their users, as well as different problems associated with their manufacture and distribution. . . . The relationship between drugs and crime is well-documented and further analysis of the impending increase in the crime rate will certainly provide further information about the negative effect narcotics have on our society. Our nation's law enforcement community, along with this Administration, the Congress and the Commission must continue to send the message to drug dealers and traffickers that the Federal government will deal harshly with those who continue to deal in drugs and engage in the violence that goes hand-in-hand with the drug trade.

Periodical Bibliography

The following articles have been selected to supplement the diverse views presented in this chapter.

Alexander Cockburn	"Dead Souls," *Nation*, April 15, 2009.
Economist	"A Voice for the Forsaken," June 11, 2009.
Gene Healy	"The Drug-War Distraction," *Orange County (CA) Register*, December 16, 2004.
Ben Johnson	"Setting Murderers Free," *FrontPage Magazine*, October 5, 2005.
Dave Kopel	"Free Plaxico Burress," *Wall Street Journal*, December 4, 2008.
Los Angeles Times	"New York's State of Mind on Drugs," April 2, 2009.
Bradford Plumer	"Rogue Wave," *New Republic*, October 16, 2007.
Harlan J. Protass	"Crack Sentencing Is Whack," *Slate*, September 28, 2007.
Julie Rawe	"Being Fair to Drug Dealers," *Time*, November 7, 2007.
San Francisco Chronicle	"Cost of 'Three Strikes' Law," March 5, 2004.
Debra J. Saunders	"The Dumb and Mean War on Drugs," *San Francisco Chronicle*, May 7, 2009.
Jacob Sullum	"Gluttons for Punishment," *Reason*, January 14, 2005.
Silja J.A. Talvi	"Incarceration Nation," *Nation*, January 5, 2007.
Stuart Taylor Jr.	"Irrational Sentencing, Top to Bottom," *Atlantic Monthly*, February 13, 2007.

Chapter 3

What Are the Effects of Mandatory Minimum Sentencing?

Chapter Preface

After a number of states and the federal government adopted mandatory minimum sentences in order to help alleviate crime and put away hardened and recidivist criminals in the 1990s, observers in the criminal justice field soon voiced a number of concerns. Many of these critics believed that mandatory minimum sentences—especially the very stringent jail terms handed out for crack cocaine possession—led to nonviolent, low-level offenders being put in jail for long periods of time. This also meant, they argued, that valuable law enforcement, court, and correctional resources were being spent on low-level drug possession charges and resulted in the prisons overcrowded with nonviolent junkies and recreational drug users instead of the high-level drug traffickers and powerful drug kingpins the laws were meant to ensnare. Observers also contended that these harsh crack cocaine possession sentencing laws also discriminated against blacks.

One of the key concerns raised about these new laws is that in formulating and implementing mandatory minimum sentences, legislators were usurping judicial power by taking the responsibility of sentencing—which is traditionally the role of the judicial branch—and placing it in the hands of prosecutors. Commentators argue that a judge with skill, experience, and wisdom can impose a sentence that takes into account mitigating circumstances of that particular case as well as relevant personal characteristics, such as the defendant's age, health status, or family responsibilities. Such a judge can pass a sentence that makes sense for that individual in light of all pertinent information. By taking away that power and imposing mandatory minimum sentences no matter what the circumstances of the offense or personal characteristics of the offender's situation, these judgments are now being made by a distant bureaucracy that ignores anything other than the offense and its prescribed punishment. Critics find this usurpation of judicial power both unjust and disturbing for American democracy.

Opponents also argue that by binding federal and state courts and individual parties to mandatory minimum sentences, the legislative branch is violating the constitutional principle of separation of powers and severing the traditional lines of political accountability in American democracy. Such a shift in responsibility would have a profound influence on the balance of powers as enshrined in the U.S. Constitution and signal a pervasive problem in American government.

The debate over the long-term consequences of mandatory minimum sentences is the focus of the viewpoints in the following chapter.

VIEWPOINT 1

"The mandatory minimum penalties for crack cocaine are not medically, scientifically or socially justifiable and result in a racially biased national drug policy."

Mandatory Minimum Sentences Discriminate Against Blacks

Jesselyn McCurdy

Jesselyn McCurdy is the legislative counsel for the American Civil Liberties Union (ACLU). In the following testimony before the U.S. Sentencing Commission, she asserts that the crack-powder cocaine sentencing disparity discriminates against blacks, particularly black men, because they comprise the vast majority of those convicted of crack cocaine offenses—despite the fact that whites and Hispanics form the majority of crack users.

As you read, consider the following questions:

1. According to McCurdy, African Americans make up what percentage of all defendants sentenced under federal crack cocaine laws?

Jesselyn McCurdy, "Testimony," U.S. Sentencing Commission Hearing on Cocaine and Sentencing Policy, November 14, 2006. Reproduced by permission of the author.

2. What percentage do whites make up of all defendants sentenced under federal crack cocaine laws, according to the author?
3. According to McCurdy, what percentage of crack users in the United States are white or Hispanic?

The disparity that exists in federal law between crack and powder cocaine sentencing continues to concern [the ACLU] due to the implications of this policy on due process and equal protection rights of all people. Equally important to our core mission are the rights of freedom of association and freedom from disproportionate punishment, which are also at risk under this sentencing regime.

The ACLU has been deeply involved in advocacy regarding race and drug policy issues for more than a decade. The ACLU assisted in convening the first national symposium in 1993 that examined the disparity in sentencing between crack and powder cocaine, which was entitled "Racial Bias in Cocaine Laws." The conclusion more than 10 years ago of the representatives from the civil rights, criminal justice, and religious organizations that participated in the Symposium was that the mandatory minimum penalties for crack cocaine are not medically, scientifically or socially justifiable and result in a racially biased national drug policy. In 2002, we urged the Commission to amend the crack guidelines to equalize crack and powder cocaine sentences at the current level for powder cocaine. Four years later, we continue to urge the Commission to support amendments to federal law that would equalize crack and powder cocaine sentences at the current level of sentences for powder cocaine.

Background and History

In June 1986, the country was shocked by the death of University of Maryland basketball star Len Bias in the midst of crack cocaine's emergence in the drug culture. Three days after being drafted by the Boston Celtics, Bias, who was African American, died of a drug and alcohol overdose. Many in the media and public assumed that Bias died of a crack overdose. Congress quickly passed the 1986 Anti-Drug Abuse Act motivated by Bias' death and in large part by the notion that the infiltration of crack cocaine was devastating America's inner cities. Although it was later revealed that Bias actually died of a powder cocaine overdose, by the time the truth about Bias' death was discovered, Congress had already passed the harsh discriminatory crack cocaine law.

Congress passed a number of mandatory minimum penalties primarily aimed at drugs and violent crime between 1984 and 1990. The most notorious mandatory minimum law enacted by Congress was the penalty relating to crack cocaine, passed as a part of the Anti-Drug Abuse Act of 1986. The little legislative history that exists suggests that members of Congress believed that crack was more addictive than powder cocaine, that it caused crime, that it caused psychosis and death, that young people were particularly prone to becoming addicted to it, and that crack's low cost and ease of manufacture would lead to even more widespread use of it. Acting upon these beliefs, Congress decided to punish use of crack more severely than use of powder cocaine.

Anti-Drug Abuse Act of 1986

On October 27, 1986, the Anti-Drug Abuse Act of 1986 was signed into law establishing the mandatory minimum sentences for federal drug trafficking crimes and creating a 100:1 sentencing disparity between powder and crack cocaine. Members of Congress intended the triggering amounts of crack to punish "major" and "serious" drug traffickers. However, the Act provided that individuals convicted of crimes involving 500 grams of powder cocaine or just 5 grams of crack (the weight of two pennies) would be sentenced to at least 5 years imprisonment, without regard to any mitigating factors. The

Demographic Characteristics of Federal Cocaine Offenders Fiscal Years 1992, 2000, and 2006

	Powder Cocaine			Crack Cocaine		
	1992 %	2000 %	2006 %	1992 %	2000 %	2006 %
Race/Ethnicity						
White	32.3	17.8	14.3	3.2	5.6	8.8
Black	27.2	30.5	27.0	91.4	84.7	81.8
Hispanic	39.8	50.8	57.5	5.3	9.0	8.4
Other	0.7	0.9	1.2	0.1	0.7	1.0
Total	100.0	100.0	100.0	100.0	100.0	100.0
Citizenship						
U.S. Citizen	67.7	63.9	60.6	91.3	93.4	96.4
Non-Citizen	32.3	36.1	39.4	8.7	6.6	3.6
Total	100.0	100.0	100.0	100.0	100.0	100.0
Gender						
Female	11.8	13.8	9.8	11.7	9.9	8.5
Male	88.2	86.2	90.2	88.3	90.1	91.5
Total	100.0	100.0	100.0	100.0	100.0	100.0
Average Age	34	34	34	28	29	31

TAKEN FROM: U.S. Sentencing Commission.

Act also provided that those individuals convicted of crimes involving 5000 grams of powder cocaine and 50 grams of crack (the weight of a candy bar) be sentenced to 10 years imprisonment.

Two years later, drug-related crimes were still on the rise. In response, Congress intensified its war against crack cocaine by passing the Omnibus Anti-Drug Abuse Act of 1988. The 1988 Act created a 5-year mandatory minimum and 20-year maximum sentence for simple possession of 5 grams or more of crack cocaine. The maximum penalty for simple possession of any amount of powder cocaine or any other drug remained at no more than 1 year in prison.

Racially Discriminatory Impact

Data on the racial disparity in the application of mandatory minimum sentences for crack cocaine is particularly disturbing. African Americans comprise the vast majority of those convicted of crack cocaine offenses, while the majority of those convicted for powder cocaine offenses are white. This is true, despite the fact that whites and Hispanics form the majority of crack users. For example, in 2003, whites constituted 7.8% and African Americans constituted more than 80% of the defendants sentenced under the harsh federal crack cocaine laws, while more than 66% of crack cocaine users in the United States are white or Hispanic. Due in large part to the sentencing disparity based on the form of the drug, African Americans serve substantially more time in prison for drug offenses than do whites. The average sentence for a crack cocaine offense in 2003, which was 123 months, was 3.5 years longer than the average sentence of 81 months for an offense involving the powder form of the drug. Also due in large part to mandatory minimum sentences for drug offenses, from 1994 to 2003, the difference between the average time African American offenders served in prison increased by 77%, compared to an increase of 28% for white drug offenders. African Americans now serve virtually as much time in prison for a drug offense at 58.7 months, as whites do for a violent offense at 61.7 months. The fact that African American defendants received the mandatory sentences more often than white defendants who were eligible for a mandatory minimum sentence, further supports the racially discriminatory impact of mandatory minimum penalties.

Over the last 20 years, federal and state drug laws and policies have also had a devastating impact on women. In 2003, 58% of all women in federal prison were convicted of drug offenses, compared to 48% of men. The growing number of women who are incarcerated disproportionately impacts African American and Hispanic women. African American women's incarceration rates for all crimes, largely driven by drug convictions, increased by 800% from 1986, compared to an increase of 400% for women of all races for the same period. Sentencing policies, particularly the mandatory minimum for low-level crack offenses, subject women who are low-level participants to the same or harsher sentences as the major dealers in a drug organization.

Consequences of Current Policy

The collateral consequences of the nation's drug policies; racially targeted prosecutions, mandatory minimums, and crack sentencing disparities have had a devastating effect on African American men, women, and families. Recent data indicates that African Americans make up only 15% of the country's drug users, yet they comprise 37% of those arrested for drug violations, 59% of those convicted, and 74% of those sentenced to prison for a drug offense. In 1986, before the enactment of federal mandatory minimum sentencing for crack cocaine offenses, the average federal drug sentence for African Americans was 11% higher than for whites. Four years later, the average federal drug sentence for African Americans was 49% higher. As law enforcement focused its efforts on crack offenses, especially those committed by African Americans, a dramatic shift occurred in the overall incarceration trends for African Americans, relative to the rest of the nation, transforming federal prisons into institutions increasingly dedicated to the African American community.

The effects of mandatory minimums not only contribute to these disproportionately high incarceration rates, but also separate fathers from families, separate mothers with sentences for minor possession crimes from their children, leave children behind in the child welfare system, create massive disfranchisement of those with felony convictions, and prohibit previously incarcerated people from receiving social services such as welfare, food stamps, and access to public housing. For example, in 2000 there were approximately 791,600 African American men in prisons and jails. That same year, there were only 603,032 African American men enrolled in higher education. The fact that there are more African American men under the jurisdiction of the penal system than in college has led scholars to conclude that our crime policies are a major contributor to the disruption of the African American family.

One of every 14 African American children has a parent locked up in prison or jail today, and African American children are 9 times more likely to have a parent incarcerated than white children. Moreover, approximately 1.4 million African American males—13% of all adult African American men—are disfranchised because of felony convictions. This represents 33% of the total disfranchised population and a rate of disfranchisement that is 7 times the national average. In addition, as a result of federal welfare legislation in 1996, there is a lifetime prohibition on the receipt of welfare for anyone convicted of a drug felony, unless a state chooses to opt out of this provision. The effect of mandatory minimums for a felony conviction, especially in the instance of simple possession or for very low-level involvement with crack cocaine, can be devastating, not just for the accused, but also for their entire family.

Dispelling the Myths

The rapid increase in the use of crack between 1984 and 1986 created many myths about the effects of the drug in popular culture. These myths were often used to justify treating crack cocaine differently from powder cocaine under federal law. For example, crack was said to cause especially violent behavior, destroy the maternal instinct leading to the abandonment of children, be a unique danger to developing fetuses, and cause a generation of so-called "crack babies" that would plague the nation's cities for their lifetimes. It was also thought to be so much more addictive than powder cocaine that it was "instantly" addicting.

In the twenty years since the enactment of the 1986 law, many of the myths surrounding crack cocaine have been dispelled, as it has become clear that there is no scientific or penological justification for the 100:1 ratio. In 1996, a study published by the *Journal of American Medical Association* (*JAMA*) found that the physiological and psychoactive effects of cocaine are similar regardless of whether it is in the form of powder or crack.

The Myth of "Crack Babies"

For instance, crack was thought to be a unique danger to developing fetuses and destroy the maternal instinct causing children to be abandoned by their mothers. During the Sentencing Commission hearings that were held prior to the release of the commission's 2002 report on Cocaine and Federal Sentencing Policy, several witnesses testified to the fact that so-called myth of "crack babies" who were thought to suffer from more pronounced developmental difficulties by their inutero exposure to the drug was not based in science. Dr. Ira J. Chasnoff, President of the Children's Research Triangle, testified before the Sentencing Commission that since the composition and effects of crack and powder cocaine are the same on the mother, the changes in the fetal brain are the same whether the mother used crack cocaine or powder cocaine.

In addition, Dr. Deborah Frank, Professor of Pediatrics at Boston University School of Medicine, in her 10-year study of the developmental and behavioral outcomes of children exposed to powder and crack cocaine in the womb, found that "the biologic thumbprints of exposure to these substances" are identical. Dr. Frank added that small but identifiable effects of prenatal exposure to powder or crack cocaine are prevalent in certain newborns' development, but they are very similar to the effects associated with prenatal tobacco exposure, such as low birth weight, height, or head circumference.

The Myth of Crack and Violence

Crack was also said to cause particularly violent behavior in those who use the drug. However, in the 2002 report on Cocaine and Federal Sentencing Policy, the Commission includes data that indicates that significantly less trafficking-related violence is associated with crack than was previously assumed. For example, in 2000: 1) 64.8% of overall crack offenses did not involve the use of a weapon by any participant in the crime; 2) 74.5% of crack offenders had no personal weapons involvement; and 3) only 2.3% of crack offenders actively used a weapon. Although by 2005 there was an increase in the percentage of crack cases that involved weapons (before the *Booker* decision 30.7% and after 27.8%), the assertion that crack physiologically causes violence has not been found to be true. Most violence associated with crack results from the nature of the illegal market for the drug and is similar to violence associated in trafficking of other drugs.

Another of the pervasive myths about crack was that it was thought to be so much more addictive than powder cocaine that it was "instantly" addicting. Crack cocaine and powder cocaine are basically the same drug, prepared differently. The 1996 *JAMA* study found that the physiological and psychoactive effects of cocaine are similar regardless of whether it is in the form of powder or crack. The study also concluded that the propensity for dependence varied by the method of ingestion, amount used and frequency, not by the form of the drug. Smoking crack or injecting powder cocaine brings about the most intense effects of cocaine. Regardless of whether a person smokes crack or uses powder cocaine, each form of the drug can be addictive. The study also indicated that people who are incarcerated for the sale or possession of cocaine, whether powder or crack, are better served by drug treatment than imprisonment.

"The bill . . . containing the crack/ powder [mandatory minimum sentencing] distinction won majority support among black congressmen, none of whom . . . objected to it as racist."

Mandatory Minimum Sentences Do Not Discriminate Against Blacks

Heather Mac Donald

Heather Mac Donald is a contributing editor of City Journal *and the John M. Olin Fellow at the Manhattan Institute. In the following viewpoint, she counters the prevailing belief that federally mandated crack cocaine penalties are racially biased. Mac Donald argues that the penalties were put in place in response to black legislators' cry for help to combat the wave of crack cocaine violence that swept through their neighborhoods in the 1980s—not a racist conspiracy to lock up disproportionate numbers of African American men.*

Heather Mac Donald, "Is the Criminal Justice System Racist?" *City Journal*, vol. 18, Spring 2006.

As you read, consider the following questions:

1. According to Mac Donald, what percentage of federal crack defendants were white and what percentage African American in 2006?
2. Why does the author believe the press has put forward a revisionist narrative on crack?
3. In 2006, what percentage of crack cocaine defendants qualified for the safety-valve provision, according to Mac Donald?

The race industry and its elite enablers take it as self-evident that high black incarceration rates result from discrimination. At a presidential primary debate this Martin Luther King Day [2008], for instance, Senator Barack Obama charged that blacks and whites "are arrested at very different rates, are convicted at very different rates, [and] receive very different sentences . . . for the same crime." Not to be outdone, Senator Hillary Clinton promptly denounced the "disgrace of a criminal-justice system that incarcerates so many more African-Americans proportionately than whites."

If a listener didn't know anything about crime, such charges of disparate treatment might seem plausible. After all, in 2006, blacks were 37.5 percent of all state and federal prisoners, though they're under 13 percent of the national population. About one in 33 black men was in prison in 2006, compared with one in 205 white men and one in 79 Hispanic men. Eleven percent of all black males between the ages of 20 and 34 are in prison or jail. The dramatic rise in the prison and jail population over the last three decades—to 2.3 million people at the end of 2007—has only amplified the racial accusations against the criminal-justice system.

The favorite culprits for high black prison rates include a biased legal system, draconian [harsh] drug enforcement, and even prison itself. None of these explanations stands up to scrutiny. The black incarceration rate is overwhelmingly a function of black crime. Insisting otherwise only worsens black alienation and further defers a real solution to the black crime problem.

Crime and Punishment

Racial activists usually remain assiduously silent about that problem. But in 2005, the black homicide rate was over seven times higher than that of whites and Hispanics combined, according to the federal Bureau of Justice Statistics. From 1976 to 2005, blacks committed over 52 percent of all murders in America. In 2006, the black arrest rate for most crimes was two to nearly three times blacks' representation in the population. Blacks constituted 39.3 percent of all violent-crime arrests, including 56.3 percent of all robbery and 34.5 percent of all aggravated-assault arrests, and 29.4 percent of all property-crime arrests.

The advocates acknowledge such crime data only indirectly: by charging bias on the part of the system's decision makers. As Obama suggested in the Martin Luther King debate, police, prosecutors, and judges treat blacks and whites differently "for the same crime."

Let's start with the idea that cops over-arrest blacks and ignore white criminals. In fact, the race of criminals reported by crime victims matches arrest data. As long ago as 1978, a study of robbery and aggravated assault in eight cities found parity between the race of assailants in victim identifications and in arrests—a finding replicated many times since, across a range of crimes. No one has ever come up with a plausible argument as to why crime victims would be biased in their reports.

Moving up the enforcement chain, the campaign against the criminal-justice system next claims that prosecutors overcharge and judges oversentence blacks. Obama describes this alleged postarrest treatment as "Scooter Libby [a politician whose felony sentence was commuted by President George W. Bush] justice for some and Jena justice for others." Jena, Louisiana, of course, was where a D.A. initially lodged attempted second-degree murder charges against black students who, in December 2006, slammed a white student's head against a concrete beam, knocking him unconscious, and then stomped and kicked him in the head while he was down. As Charlotte Allen has brilliantly chronicled in *The Weekly Standard*, a local civil rights activist crafted a narrative linking the attack to an unrelated incident months earlier, in which three white students hung two nooses from a schoolyard tree—a display that may or may not have been intended as a racial provocation. This entrepreneur then embellished the tale with other alleged instances of redneck racism—above all, the initial attempted-murder charges. An enthusiastic national press responded to the bait exactly as intended, transforming the "Jena Six" into victims rather than perpetrators. In the seven months of ensuing headlines and protests, Jena became a symbol of systemic racial unfairness in America's court system. If blacks were disproportionately in prison, the refrain went, it was because they faced biased prosecutors—like the one in Jena—as well as biased juries and judges.

A Different Conclusion

Backing up this bias claim has been the holy grail of criminology for decades—and the prize remains as elusive as ever. In 1997, criminologists Robert Sampson and Janet Lauritsen reviewed the massive literature on charging and sentencing. They concluded that "large racial differences in criminal offending," not racism, explained why more blacks were in prison proportionately than whites and for longer terms. A 1987 analysis of Georgia felony convictions, for example, found that blacks frequently received disproportionately lenient punishment. A 1990 study of 11,000 California cases found that slight racial disparities in sentence length resulted

Drug Offenders in State Prison by Race/Ethnicity, 1999–2005

	1999	2000	2001	2002	2003	2004	2005	Change, 99–05
All Drug Offenders	251,200	251,100	246,100	265,000	250,900	249,400	253,300	0.8%
White #	50,700	58,200	57,300	64,500	64,800	65,900	72,300	42.6%
White %	20.2%	23.2%	23.3%	24.3%	25.9%	26.4%	28.5%	
Black #	144,700	145,300	139,700	126,000	133,100	112,500	113,500	−21.6%
Black %	57.6%	57.9%	56.8%	47.5%	53%	45.1%	44.8%	
Hispanic #	52,100	43,300	47,000	61,700	50,100	51,800	51,100	−1.9%
Hispanic %	20.7%	17.2%	19.1%	23.3%	20%	20.8%	20.2%	

TAKEN FROM: The Sentencing Project, April 2009.

from blacks' prior records and other legally relevant variables. A 1994 Justice Department survey of felony cases from the country's 75 largest urban areas discovered that blacks actually had a lower chance of prosecution following a felony than whites did and that they were less likely to be found guilty at trial. Following conviction, blacks were more likely to receive prison sentences, however—an outcome that reflected the gravity of their offenses as well as their criminal records.

Another criminologist—easily as liberal as Sampson—reached the same conclusion in 1995: "Racial differences in patterns of offending, not racial bias by police and other officials, are the principal reason that such greater proportions of blacks than whites are arrested, prosecuted, convicted and imprisoned," Michael Tonry wrote in *Malign Neglect*. (Tonry did go on to impute malign racial motives to drug enforcement, however.) The media's favorite criminologist, Alfred Blumstein, found in 1993 that blacks were significantly underrepresented in prison for homicide compared with their presence in arrest.

This consensus hasn't made the slightest dent in the ongoing search for systemic racism. An entire industry in the law schools now dedicates itself to flushing out prosecutorial and judicial bias, using ever more complicated statistical artillery. The net result? A few new studies show tiny, unexplained racial disparities in sentencing, while other analyses continue to find none.

Any differences that do show up are trivially small compared with the exponentially greater rates of criminal offending among blacks. No criminologist would claim, moreover, to have controlled for every legal factor that affects criminal-justice outcomes, says Patrick Langan, former senior statistician for the Bureau of Justice Statistics. Prosecutors and judges observe the heinousness of a defendant's conduct, for example, but a number-crunching researcher has no easy way to discover and quantify that variable.

Some criminologists replace statistics with High Theory in their search for racism. The criminal-justice system does treat individual suspects and criminals equally, they concede. But the problem is how society *defines* crime and criminals. Crime is a social construction designed to marginalize minorities, these theorists argue. A liberal use of scare quotes is virtually mandatory in such discussions, to signal one's distance from primitive notions like "law-abiding" and "dangerous." Arguably, vice crimes are partly definitional (though even there, the law enforcement system focuses on them to the extent that they harm communities). But the social constructivists are talking about all crime, and it's hard to see how one could "socially reconstruct" assault or robbery so as to convince victims that they haven't been injured.

The War on Drugs

Unfair drug policies are an equally popular explanation for black incarceration rates. Legions of pundits, activists, and academics charge that the war on drugs is a war on minorities—a de facto war at best, an intentional one at worst.

Playing a starring role in this conceit are federal crack penalties, the source of the greatest amount of misinformation in the race and incarceration debate. Crack is a smokeable and highly addictive cocaine concentrate, created by cooking powder cocaine until it hardens into pellets called "rocks." Crack produces a faster—and more potent—high than powder cocaine, and it's easier to use, since smoking avoids the unpleasantness of needles and is more efficient than snorting. Under the 1986 federal Anti-Drug Abuse Act, getting caught with five grams of crack carries a mandatory minimum five-year sentence in federal court; to trigger the same five-year minimum, powder-cocaine traffickers would have to get caught with 500 grams. On average, federal crack sentences are three to six times longer than powder sentences for equivalent amounts.

The media love to target the federal crack penalties because crack defendants are likely to be black. In 2006, 81 percent of federal crack defendants were black, while only 27 percent of federal powder-cocaine defendants were. Since federal crack rules are more severe than those for powder, and crack offenders are disproportionately black, those rules must explain why so many blacks are in prison, the conventional wisdom holds.

Look at the Numbers

But consider the actual number of crack sellers sentenced in federal court each year. In 2006, 5,619 were tried federally, 4,495 of them black. From 1996 to 2000, the federal courts sentenced more powder traffickers (23,743) than crack traffickers (23,121). It's going to take a lot more than 5,000 or so crack defendants a year to account for the 562,000 black prisoners in state and federal facilities at the end of 2006—or the 858,000 black prisoners in custody overall, if one includes the population of county and city jails. Nor do crack/powder disparities at the state level explain black incarceration rates: only 13 states distinguish between crack and powder sentences, and they employ much smaller sentence differentials.

The press almost never mentions the federal methamphetamine-trafficking penalties, which are identical to those for crack: five grams of meth net you a mandatory minimum five-year sentence. In 2006, the 5,391 sentenced federal meth defendants (nearly as many as the crack defendants) were 54 percent white, 39 percent Hispanic, and 2 percent black. But no one calls the federal meth laws anti-Hispanic or anti-white.

Crack Penalties Under Scrutiny

Nevertheless, the federal crack penalties dominate discussions on race and incarceration because they seem to provide a concrete example of egregious racial disparity. This leads to a commonly expressed syllogism: crack penalties have a disparate impact on blacks; disparate impact is racist; therefore, crack penalties are racist. This syllogism has been particularly prominent recently, thanks to the U.S. Sentencing Commission's 2007 decision to lighten federal crack penalties retroactively in the name of racial equity.

The press has covered this development voraciously, serving up a massive dose of crack revisionism aimed at proving the racist origins of the war on crack. Crack was never a big deal, the revisionist story line goes. But when Boston Celtics draft pick Len Bias died of a crack overdose in 1986, the media went into overdrive covering the crack phenomenon. "Images—or perhaps anecdotes—about the evils of crack, and the street crime it was presumed to stoke" circulated, as the *New York Times* archly put it in a December 2007 article. A "moral panic" (Michael Tonry's term) ensued about an imaginary threat from a powerless minority group. Whites feared that addicted blacks would invade their neighborhoods. Sensational stories about "crack babies" surfaced. All this hysteria resulted in the unnecessary federal crack penalties.

Since the 1980s, the revisionist narrative continues, experts have determined that powder and crack show more pharmacological "similarities than differences," in the *Times*'s words, and that crack is no more damaging to fetuses than alcohol. The belief that crack was an inner-city scourge was thus a racist illusion, and the sentencing structure to quell it a racist assault. Or, as U.S. District Judge Clyde Cahill put it, in what one hopes is not a representative sample of the federal judicial temperament: "Legislators' unconscious racial aversion towards blacks, sparked by unsubstantiated reports of the effects of crack, reactionary media prodding, and an agitated constituency, motivated the legislators . . . to produce a dual system of punishment."

A Revisionist Narrative

Leave aside the irony of the press's now declaring smugly that the press exaggerated the ravages of crack. (The same *New*

York Times that now sneers at "images—or perhaps anecdotes—about the evils of crack" ran searing photos of crack addicts in 1993 that included a woman kneeling before a crack dealer, unzipping his fly, a baby clinging to her back; such degraded prostitutes, known as "strawberries," were pervasive casualties of the epidemic.) The biggest problem with the revisionist narrative is its unreality. The assertion that concern about crack resulted from "unconscious racial aversion towards blacks" ignores a key fact: black leaders were the first to sound the alarm about the drug, as Harvard law professor Randall Kennedy documents in *Race, Crime, and the Law*. Harlem congressman Charles Rangel initiated the federal response to the epidemic, warning the House of Representatives in March 1986 that crack had made cocaine "frightening[ly]" accessible to youth. A few months later, Brooklyn congressman Major Owens explicitly rejected what is now received wisdom about media hype. "None of the press accounts really have exaggerated what is actually going on," Owens said; the crack epidemic was "as bad as any articles have stated." Queens congressman Alton Waldon then called on his colleagues to act: "For those of us who are black this self-inflicted pain is the worst oppression we have known since slavery. . . . Let us . . . pledge to crack down on crack." The bill that eventually passed, containing the crack/powder distinction, won majority support among black congressmen, none of whom, as Kennedy points out, objected to it as racist.

These politicians were reacting to a devastating outbreak of inner-city violence and addiction unleashed by the new form of cocaine. Because crack came in small, easily digestible amounts, it democratized what had been a rarefied drug, making an intense high available to people with very little money. The crack market differed radically from the discreet phone transactions and private deliveries that characterized powder-cocaine distribution: volatile young dealers sold crack on street corners, using guns to establish their turf. Crack, homicides, and assaults went hand in hand; certain areas of New York became "like a war zone," retired DEA special agent Robert Stutman told PBS's *Frontline* in 2000. The large national spike in violence in the mid-1980s was largely due to the crack trade, and its victims were overwhelmingly black inner-city residents.

Though the elites are furiously rewriting crack history, many people who lived through it are not. In April 2007, Los Angeles prosecutor Robert Grace won the conviction of a crack dealer who had raped and strangled to death ten strawberries between 1987 and 1998. The "crack epidemic was one of the worst things that happened to the black and brown community," Grace asserts. Matthew Kennedy managed an infamous public housing project in Watts during the crack epidemic. "Some of us remember how bad it was," he says. When children avoid school for fear of getting shot by drug gangs, "you've just lost that generation." Lawrence Tolliver has witnessed his share of shootings outside his South Central barbershop. "Sometimes it was so bad you had to scout the horizon like a gazelle at a watering hole in Africa," he recalls.

It takes shameless sleight of hand to turn an effort to protect blacks into a conspiracy against them. If Congress had ignored black legislators' calls to increase cocaine-trafficking penalties, the outcry among the groups now crying racism would have been deafening. Yes, a legislative bidding war drove federal crack penalties ultimately to an arbitrary and excessive point; the reduction of those penalties is appropriate. But what led to the crack-sentencing scheme wasn't racism but legal logic. Prosecutors rely on heavy statutory penalties to induce defendants to spill the beans on their criminal colleagues. "An amazing public spirit is engendered when you tell someone he is facing 150 years to life but has the possibility of getting out after eight if he tells you who committed a string of homicides," says Walter Arsenault, who headed the Manhattan district attorney's homicide-investigation unit in the 1980s and 1990s.

Myth of the Low-Level Offender

Race activists endlessly promote the claim that the draconian federal crack laws are sweeping up mere sad sacks with a little extra crack to spare. But anyone who fits that description is exempt from the federal sentencing scheme. Traffickers with only a modest criminal history who didn't injure others or have a gun when arrested can escape the mandatory federal sentences if they don't lie to the government about their offense (there is no requirement to rat out others). In 2006, only 15.4 percent of crack-cocaine defendants qualified for this safety-valve provision, compared with 48.4 percent of powder-cocaine offenders; in 2000, even fewer crack defendants qualified—12.6 percent. Crack sellers seldom merit the escape clause because their criminal histories tend to be much more severe than powder sellers' and because they're more likely to have or use weapons. The congressional distinction between crack and powder sellers, it turns out, had a firm grounding.

Equally misleading is the criticism that few crack "kingpins" can be found in federal prison. This is not surprising, because "kingpins" in the traditional sense—heads of major drug-importing rings—don't exist in the crack world. Crack is not imported but cooked up locally. Its supply and distribution scheme is more horizontal than vertical, unlike that of powder cocaine and heroin. Federal crack enforcement wasn't about stopping the flow of illegal drugs into the country; it was about stopping urban violence. And that violence was coming from street dealers.

Myths About Drugs

Critics follow up their charges about crack with several empirical claims about drugs and imprisonment. None is true. The first is that drug enforcement has been the most important cause of the overall rising incarceration rate since the 1980s. Yet even during the most rapid period of population growth in prisons—from 1980 to 1990—36 percent of the growth in state prisons (where 88 percent of the nation's prisoners are housed) came from violent crimes, compared with 33 percent from drug crimes. Since then, drug offenders have played an even smaller role in state prison expansion. From 1990 to 2000, violent offenders accounted for 53 percent of the census increase—and all of the increase from 1999 to 2004.

Next, critics blame drug enforcement for rising racial disparities in prison. Again, the facts say otherwise. In 2006, blacks were 37.5 percent of the 1,274,600 state prisoners. If you remove drug prisoners from that population, the percentage of black prisoners drops to 37 percent—half of a percentage point, hardly a significant difference. (No criminologist, to the best of my knowledge, has ever performed this exercise.)

The rise of drug cases in the criminal-justice system has been dramatic, it's important to acknowledge. In 1979, drug offenders were 6.4 percent of the state prison population; in 2004, they were 20 percent. Even so, violent and property offenders continue to dominate the ranks: in 2004, 52 percent of state prisoners were serving time for violence and 21 percent for property crimes, for a combined total over three and a half times that of state drug offenders. In federal prisons, drug offenders went from 25 percent of all federal inmates in 1980 to 47.6 percent of all federal inmates in 2006. Drug-war opponents focus almost exclusively on federal, as opposed to state, prisons because the proportion of drug offenders is highest there. But the federal system held just 12.3 percent of the nation's prisoners in 2006.

Viewpoint 3

"It would be an enormous economic stimulus if we stopped wasting so much money arresting and locking people up for non-violent drug offenses."

Mandatory Minimum Drug Sentences Waste Resources

Kevin Zeese

Kevin Zeese is a writer and political activist who has worked to reform U.S. drug policy. In the following viewpoint, he argues that draconian, or exceedingly harsh, sentences for low-level drug offenders are a tragic waste of resources. Zeese outlines wrong-headed approaches that various presidents and government officials have taken to the issue, and fears that President Barack Obama is also going down the wrong path regarding the war on drugs.

As you read, consider the following questions:

1. What are the Rockefeller drug laws, according to the author?
2. How much does Zeese estimate that it costs New York to imprison drug offenders?

Kevin Zeese, "Escaping the Drug War Quagmire," *Counterpunch*, April 8, 2009.

3. According to the author, what percentage of the world's prisoners are imprisoned in the United States?

The passage of major reforms in the Rockefeller drug laws last week [first week of April 2009]—the notorious 1973 mandatory sentencing laws that filled New York's prisons but have not prevented long-term growing drug-related problems—demonstrates the challenge the United States faces in getting out of the drug war trap.

The Rockefeller Legacy

Nelson Rockefeller served as governor of New York from 1959 to 1973. He spent millions in attempts to win the Republican presidential nomination in 1960, 1964, and 1968 and became Vice President in 1974. Rockefeller was known as a liberal Republican in a party led by people like Barry Goldwater and Richard Nixon.

The Rockefeller drug laws—the toughest drug laws in the United States—allowed him to be a tough on drugs politician and respond to Nixon's call for a "war on drugs." The mandatory minimum sentences, which covered all illegal drugs from marijuana to heroin, treated possession of over 56 grams as the equivalent of second degree murder.

There are nearly 12,000 people in New York's prisons incarcerated under the drug laws, most of them minor offenders with no history of violent behavior. It costs New York $520 million a year to imprison them. Almost 90% of those locked up in New York for drug offenses are African American or Latino, despite research showing that the vast majority of people who use and sell drugs are white.

Over thirty-five years the laws cost the state billions of dollars and ruined tens of thousands of lives. And, throughout the time New York saw one drug crisis after another—the cocaine-crack era, multi-generational heroin addiction, a wave of HIV/AIDS related to drug use, drug-trafficking related

Federal Corrections Costs Soared in Last 25 Years

Federal correctional costs increased 925 percent from 1982 to 2007, to over $5.4 billion.

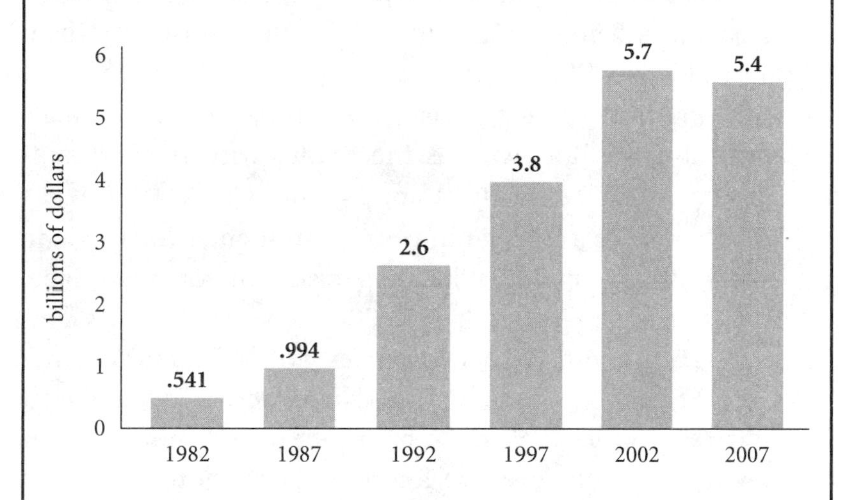

TAKEN FROM: Bureau of Justice Statistics, U.S. Dept. of Justice, Justice Expenditure and Employment in the United States, 2003, Office of Management and Budget, Dept. of Justice Budget Information.

crime waves and consistent high levels of overdose deaths. The Rockefeller drug laws were a costly failure but it took decades to even make modest reforms.

Indeed, full repeal of the laws is still opposed, especially by upstate legislators who profit from the prison-industrial complex. The reforms enacted still leave mandatory sentences on the books, but give judges discretion in some cases to require treatment instead of incarceration. Only 1,800 people will be affected by the change because of compromises between the New York State Senate and House.

Nixon and the Drug War

Rockefeller recalls another drug war Republican—Richard Nixon who set the modern drug war trap. When he was president the National Commission on Marijuana and Drug Abuse recommended an alternative path: treat hard drugs as a public health issue and do not treat possession, personal cultivation and non-profit transfer of marijuana as crimes. White House tapes reveal Nixon reacting negatively to the suggestions based on racism, anti-Semitism and hatred for the educated (Nixon to Bob Haldeman: "... every one of the bastards that are out for legalizing marijuana is Jewish. What the Christ is the matter with the Jews, Bob, what is the matter with them? I suppose it's because most of them are psychiatrists ...")

In response to the unanimous recommendations, Nixon upped the drug war ante, with a special focus on marijuana. Marijuana arrests increased by 100,000 the year after the Commission recommended such offenses not be a crime. And, now, the FBI reports that in 2007 there were 872,720 marijuana arrests—more than for rape, robbery and murder combined—and 90% of those are for mere possession. This for a substance that nearly half the country believes should be legal.

How is there any legitimacy in a law that is so widely opposed resulting in hundreds of thousands of arrests annually? No wonder the United States has the embarrassment of incarcerating 25% of the world's prisoners while having only 5% of the world's population.

America vs. the Netherlands

An interesting parallel with the American experience is the experience of another country that in the same year had a national commission report which made very similar recommendations. The difference, at the outset, unlike Nixon, their leaders put in place the recommendations of the commission. Today, the Netherlands has one half the marijuana use rate per capita, one-third the heroin use and one-quarter the cocaine use. In addition, their prison population is one-seventh that of the United States.

The facts are on the side of those who advocate ending the drug war, but breaking free of this failed policy has been extremely challenging. Democrats, who many hope would be the alternative to the Just Say No Republican Party, have consistently been afraid to tackle the issue. President [Bill] Clinton outflanked the Republicans by putting a general in charge of drug policy.

Obama's Approach

President [Barack] Obama, who supported decriminalization while in the Illinois State Senate, mocked a question about ending the marijuana war at a recent web town hall meeting. Obama fielded the most popular questions sent to the White House website where 3.5 million people voted. Marijuana legalization was No. 1 on the list. Obama said:

> "I have to say that there was one question that was voted on that ranked fairly high, and that was whether legalizing marijuana would improve the economy and job creation... I don't know what that says about the online audience... We want to make sure that it was answered. The answer is, no, I don't think that is a good strategy to grow our economy."

Jack Cole, the executive director of Law Enforcement Against Prohibition, a group representing thousands of former law enforcement officers opposed to the drug war, said: "Despite the president's flippant comments today, the grievous harms of marijuana prohibition are no laughing matter. It would be an enormous economic stimulus if we stopped wasting so much money arresting and locking people up for nonviolent drug offenses and instead brought in new tax revenue from legal sales, just as we did when we ended alcohol prohibition 75 years ago during the Great Depression."

Obama picked as vice president Joe Biden, who as Chairman of the Judiciary Committee put in place mandatory minimum sentences, the harsh disparity between crack and powder cocaine sentencing and the drug czar's office among other drug war measures. His chief of staff, Rahm Emanuel, also favors a tough on drugs approach. However, the president did announce he is stopping the waste of federal resources on medical marijuana prosecutions and supports needle exchange to prevent HIV/AIDS. In addition, he has appointed the police chief of Seattle, a city that has put in significant drug policy reforms, as his drug czar.

The Wrong Approach

And, President Obama is facing an aggressive drug war in Mexico where more than 7,000 have been killed in the last 18 months. This would be a good opportunity for the president to point out how violence is one of the side effects of prohibiting drugs. Many cities in the U.S. have seen more prohibition-related violence then Chicago saw during alcohol prohibition. But, instead Obama is mocking the issue and calling out National Guard troops.

Militarization of the drug war on the Mexican border is something that previous presidents have tried and it has always backfired. President Nixon put in place Operation Intercept, searching one out of three cars and trucks crossing the border. The result, marijuana and heroin traffickers switched to air, sea and commerce causing a heroin and marijuana glut. President [Ronald] Reagan used the military to intercept boats and planes bringing marijuana into the United States. The result, traffickers switched to the more profitable and easier to smuggle cocaine, causing the cocaine decade of the 1980s. President Clinton used the Marines on the border until they shot and killed a high school student in his backyard while he was herding goats for the town's cheese co-operative.

What disaster will Obama bring by failing to confront the root cause questions: should drug prohibition continue, does the drug war work, are its costs greater than its benefits and is there a better way forward?

VIEWPOINT 4

"[Mandatory minimum] sentences are entirely appropriate in light of the plight of drug-endangered children."

Mandatory Minimum Drug Sentences Protect Children

Catherine M. O'Neil

Catherine M. O'Neil was associate deputy attorney general and director of the Organized Crime Drug Enforcement Task Forces when she gave the following congressional testimony. In her statement she expresses the support of the U.S. Justice Department for mandatory minimum sentences for any drug offender who endangers children through exposure to drug activity, sells drugs to children, or uses minors in drug trafficking. O'Neil argues that the mandatory minimum sentences for such offenders proposed in H.R. 4547, Defending America's Most Vulnerable: Safe Access to Drug Treatment and Child Protection Act of 2004, are appropriate and justified.

Catherine M. O'Neil, "Defending America's Most Vulnerable: Safe Access to Drug Treatment and Child Protection Act of 2005," Hearing Before the Subcommittee on Crime, Terrorism, and Homeland Security of the Committee of the Judiciary, House of Representatives, April 12, 2005.

As you read, consider the following questions:

1. In 2003–2004, how many convictions were there of people engaged in drug activity involving minors, according to O'Neil?
2. According to the author, how many defendants were sentenced annually between 1998 and 2002 under the guideline that provides stronger penalties for selling to minors?
3. Why does O'Neil believe that mandatory minimum sentences are better than sentencing guidelines in appropriate circumstances?

Protecting vulnerable victims from drug dealing predators, particularly those who would exploit human weakness by preying on persons afflicted with addictions to drugs or on those who, because of their youth and immaturity, are particularly susceptible to influence, is a laudable goal and one the Department of Justice fully endorses. [In 2004], Congress made significant strides by enacting the PROTECT Act, a law that has proved effective in enabling law enforcement to pursue and to punish wrongdoers who threaten the youth of America.

The Act now under consideration takes Congress' commendable efforts even further by focusing on the scourge of drug trafficking in some of its most base and dangerous forms: trafficking to minors or in places where they may congregate, and trafficking in or near drug treatment centers.

Drugs Endanger Children

Endangerment of children through exposure to drug activity, sales of drugs to children, the use of minors in drug trafficking, and the peddling of pharmaceutical and other illicit drugs to drug treatment patients are all significant problems today.

One need only consider the following few examples:

- In 2003, 3,625 children were found in the approximately 9,000 methamphetamine laboratories seized nationwide. Of those, 1,040 children were physically present at the clandestine labs and 906 actually resided at the lab site premises. Forty-one children found were injured. Law enforcement referred 501 children to child protective services following the enforcement activity.
- According to the BBC [British Broadcasting Corporation], a 12-year-old drug mule living in Nigeria swallowed 87 condoms full of heroin before boarding a flight from London to New York. He was offered $1,900 to make the trip.
- In "Operation Paris Express," an investigation led by the former U.S. Customs Service, agents learned that members of the targeted international drug trafficking organization specifically instructed couriers to use juveniles for smuggling trips to allay potential suspicions by U.S. Customs. On one smuggling trip, two couriers, posing as a couple, brought a mentally handicapped teenager with them while they carried 200,000 Ecstasy pills concealed in socks in their luggage.
- More recently, "Operation Kids for Cover," an Organized Crime Drug Enforcement Task Force (OCDETF) investigation in Chicago and elsewhere, uncovered a cocaine smuggling group that "rented" infants to accompany couriers, many of whom were drug addicts themselves, who were transporting liquified cocaine in baby formula containers.
- In Vermont, prosecutors convicted drug dealer Michael Baker for selling cocaine to, among others, high-schoolers. A sophomore honors student who got cocaine from Baker began using extensively and started

Monitoring the Future Study: Trends in Prevalence of Various Drugs for 8th-Graders, 10th-Graders, and 12th-Graders

*2005–2008 (in percent)**

	8th-Graders				10th-Graders				12th-Graders			
	2005	**2006**	**2007**	**2008**	**2005**	**2006**	**2007**	**2008**	**2005**	**2006**	**2007**	**2008**
Any Illicit Drug Use												
Lifetime	21.4	20.9	[19.0]	**19.6**	38.2	36.1	35.6	**34.1**	50.4	48.2	46.8	**47.4**
Past Year	15.5	14.8	[13.2]	**14.1**	29.8	28.7	28.1	**26.9**	38.4	36.5	35.9	**36.6**
Past Month	8.5	8.1	7.4	**7.6**	17.3	16.8	16.9	**15.8**	23.1	21.5	21.9	**22.3**
Marijuana/Hashish												
Lifetime	16.5	15.7	14.2	**14.6**	34.1	31.8	31.0	**29.9**	44.8	42.3	41.8	**42.6**
Past Year	12.2	11.7	[10.3]	**10.9**	26.6	25.2	24.6	**23.9**	33.6	31.5	31.7	**32.4**
Past Month	6.6	6.5	5.7	**5.8**	15.2	14.2	14.2	**13.8**	19.8	18.3	18.8	**19.4**
Daily	1.0	1.0	0.8	**0.9**	3.1	2.8	2.8	**2.7**	5.0	5.0	5.1	**5.4**
Inhalants												
Lifetime	17.1	16.1	15.6	**15.7**	13.1	13.3	13.6	**12.8**	11.4	11.1	10.5	**9.9**
Past Year	9.5	9.1	8.3	**8.9**	6.0	6.5	6.6	**5.9**	5.0	4.5	3.7	**3.8**
Past Month	4.2	4.1	3.9	**4.1**	2.2	2.3	2.5	**2.1**	2.0	1.5	1.2	**1.4**
Hallucinogens												
Lifetime	3.8	3.4	3.1	**3.3**	5.8	6.1	6.4	**5.5**	8.8	8.3	8.4	**8.7**
Past Year	2.4	2.1	1.9	**2.1**	4.0	4.1	4.4	**3.9**	5.5	4.9	5.4	**5.9**
Past Month	1.1	0.9	1.0	**0.9**	1.5	1.5	1.7	**1.3**	1.9	1.5	1.7	**[2.2]**

continued

Monitoring the Future Study: Trends in Prevalence of Various Drugs for 8th-Graders, 10th-Graders, and 12th-Graders [CONTINUED]

*2005–2008 (in percent)**

	8th-Graders				10th-Graders				12th-Graders			
	2005	2006	2007	2008	2005	2006	2007	2008	2005	2006	2007	2008
LSD												
Lifetime	1.9	1.6	1.6	**1.9**	2.5	2.7	3.0	**2.6**	3.5	3.3	3.4	**4.0**
Past Year	1.2	0.9	1.1	**1.3**	1.5	1.7	1.9	**1.8**	1.8	1.7	2.1	**2.7**
Past Month	0.5	0.4	0.5	**0.5**	0.6	0.7	0.7	**0.7**	0.7	0.6	0.6	**[1.1]**
Cocaine												
Lifetime	3.7	3.4	3.1	**3.0**	5.2	4.8	5.3	**4.5**	8.0	8.5	7.8	**7.2**
Past Year	2.2	2.0	2.0	**1.8**	3.5	3.2	3.4	**3.0**	5.1	5.7	5.2	**4.4**
Past Month	1.0	1.0	0.9	**0.8**	1.5	1.5	1.3	**1.2**	2.3	2.5	[2.0]	**1.9**
Crack Cocaine												
Lifetime	2.4	2.3	2.1	**2.0**	2.5	2.2	2.3	**2.0**	3.5	3.5	3.2	**2.8**
Past Year	1.4	1.3	1.3	**1.1**	1.7	1.3	1.3	**1.3**	1.9	2.1	1.9	**[1.6]**
Past Month	0.6	0.6	0.6	**0.5**	0.7	0.7	[0.5]	**0.5**	1.0	0.9	0.9	**0.8**
Heroin												
Lifetime	1.5	1.4	1.3	**1.4**	1.5	1.4	1.5	**[1.2]**	1.5	1.4	1.5	**1.3**
Past Year	0.8	0.8	0.8	**0.9**	0.9	0.9	0.8	**0.8**	0.8	0.8	0.9	**0.7**
Past Month	0.5	0.3	0.4	**0.4**	0.5	0.5	0.4	**0.4**	0.5	0.4	0.4	**0.4**

continued

Monitoring the Future Study: Trends in Prevalence of Various Drugs for 8th-Graders, 10th-Graders, and 12th-Graders [CONTINUED]

*2005–2008 (in percent)**

	8th-Graders				10th-Graders				12th-Graders			
	2005	2006	2007	2008	2005	2006	2007	2008	2005	2006	2007	2008
Tranquilizers												
Lifetime	4.1	4.3	3.9	**3.9**	7.1	7.2	7.4	**6.8**	9.9	10.3	9.5	**8.9**
Past Year	2.8	2.6	2.4	**2.4**	4.8	5.2	5.3	**4.6**	6.8	6.6	6.2	**6.2**
Past Month	1.3	1.3	1.1	**1.2**	2.3	2.4	2.6	**[1.9]**	2.9	2.7	2.6	**2.6**
MDMA												
Lifetime	2.8	2.5	2.3	**2.4**	4.0	4.5	5.2	**4.3**	5.4	6.5	6.5	**6.2**
Past Year	1.7	1.4	1.5	**1.7**	2.6	2.8	3.5	**2.9**	3.0	4.1	4.5	**4.3**
Past Month	0.6	0.7	0.6	**0.8**	1.0	1.2	1.2	**1.1**	1.0	1.3	1.6	**1.8**
Methamphetamine												
Lifetime	3.1	2.7	[1.8]	**2.3**	4.1	3.2	2.8	**2.4**	4.5	4.4	[3.0]	**2.8**
Past Year	1.8	1.8	[1.1]	**1.2**	2.9	1.8	1.6	**1.5**	2.5	2.5	[1.7]	**1.2**
Past Month	0.7	0.6	0.6	**0.7**	1.1	0.7	0.4	**[0.7]**	0.9	0.9	0.6	**0.6**
Vicodin												
Past Year	2.6	3.0	2.7	**2.9**	5.9	7.0	7.2	**6.7**	9.5	9.7	9.6	**9.7**

continued

Monitoring the Future Study: Trends in Prevalence of Various Drugs for 8th-Graders, 10th-Graders, and 12th-Graders [CONTINUED]

*2005–2008 (in percent)**

	8th-Graders				10th-Graders				12th-Graders			
	2005	**2006**	**2007**	**2008**	**2005**	**2006**	**2007**	**2008**	**2005**	**2006**	**2007**	**2008**
OxyContin												
Past Year	1.8	2.6	1.8	**2.1**	3.2	3.8	3.9	**3.6**	5.5	4.3	5.2	**4.7**
Cough Medicine (non-prescription)*												
Past Year	—	4.2	4.0	**3.6**	—	5.3	5.4	**5.3**	—	6.9	5.8	**5.5**

*Data in brackets indicate statistically significant change from the previous year.
** A question on the past year abuse of non-prescription cough medicine was added in 2006.

TAKEN FROM: National Institute on Drug Abuse, 2008.

referring friends from his peer group to Baker in exchange for drugs. This honors student never returned to high school for his junior year.

- As reported in the *Washington Post*, between 2000 and 2002, more than 200 persons were arrested here in Washington, D.C., for distributing diverted prescription drugs and other illicit drugs in a parking lot that abuts one of D.C.'s largest methadone clinics and is within three blocks of several other treatment facilities. The dealers in that open air market took advantage of the drug treatment patients—enticing them with illicit substances and undermining any progress that had been made on their road to recovery.

The Department of Justice is committed to vigorously prosecuting drug trafficking in all of its egregious forms, whether it be a top-level international narcotics supplier or a street-level predator who tempts a child or an addict with the lure of intoxication or the promise of profit.

Successes in the War on Drugs

We have had some successes. Statistics maintained by the Department of Justice Executive Office for United States Attorneys indicate that, in the last two years alone [2003 and 2004], we have had over 400 convictions under Title 21, Sections 859, 860 and 861, of persons engaged in drug activity involving minors. Moreover, statistics maintained by the U.S. Sentencing Commission indicate that, between 1998 and 2002, approximately 300 defendants were sentenced annually under the guideline that provides for enhanced penalties for drug activity involving minors or in protected locations. But our tools are limited. And we have no specific weapon against those who distribute controlled substances within the vicinity of a drug treatment center.

The people who would sink to the depths of inhumanity by targeting their trafficking activity at those with the least ability to resist such offers are deserving not only of our most pointed contempt, but, more importantly, of severe punishment. The Department of Justice cannot and will not tolerate this conduct in a free and safe America, and that is why the Department of Justice stands firmly behind the intent of this legislation to increase the punishment meted out to those who would harm us, our children, and those seeking to escape the cycle of addiction.

Mandatory Minimum Sentences

I would like to spend a few minutes talking specially about mandatory minimum sentences and, in particular, the mandatory minimum sentence provisions of H.R. 4547.

The Justice Department supports mandatory minimum sentences in appropriate circumstances. In a way sentencing guidelines cannot, mandatory minimum statutes provide a level of uniformity and predictability in sentencing. They deter certain types of criminal behavior determined by Congress to be sufficiently egregious as to merit harsh penalties by clearly forewarning the potential offender and the public at large of the minimum potential consequences of committing such an offense. And mandatory minimum sentences can also incapacitate dangerous offenders for long periods of time, thereby increasing public safety. Equally importantly, mandatory minimum sentences provide an indispensable tool for prosecutors, because they provide the strongest incentive to defendants to cooperate against the others who were involved in their criminal activity.

Key Tool for Prosecutors

In drug cases, where the ultimate goal is to rid society of the entire trafficking enterprise, mandatory minimum statutes are especially significant. Unlike a bank robbery, for which a bank teller or an ordinary citizen could be a critical witness, typically in drug cases the only witnesses are drug users and/or other drug traffickers. The offer of relief from a mandatory minimum sentence in exchange for truthful testimony allows the Government to move steadily and effectively up the chain of supply, using the lesser distributors to prosecute the more serious dealers and their leaders and suppliers.

The Department thinks that mandatory minimum sentences are needed in appropriate circumstances, and we support the specific mandatory minimum sentences proposed in H.R. 4547. These sentences are entirely appropriate in light of the plight of drug-endangered children throughout this country.

VIEWPOINT 5

"[The U.S. Sentencing Commission] has usurped much of the judiciary's traditional authority over sentencing through its enactment of mandatory Guidelines."

Mandatory Minimum Sentences Usurp Judicial Power

Erik Luna

Erik Luna was a state prosecutor and Fulbright scholar on sentencing alternatives and is currently a law professor at Washington and Lee University in Virginia. In the following viewpoint, Luna maintains that mandatory sentencing and the sentencing guidelines have usurped the power of the judiciary and handed it over to a bureaucracy. Luna contends that this rigid sentencing system discounts the skill, wisdom, and experience accrued by members of the judiciary and leads to judges, prosecutors, and defense attorneys maneuvering to avoid the prescribed consequences of the mandatory sentencing.

Erik Luna, "Misguided Guidelines," Cato Institute, Policy Analysis, November 2, 2005.

As you read, consider the following questions:

1. Why does Luna link the sentencing guidelines and mandatory minimum sentences together?
2. In a 1992 poll, as cited by the author, how many federal judges believed that the current sentencing system should be completely eliminated?
3. What does Luna recommend to fix the system?

Fifteen years ago [in 1987], the federal justice system underwent a revolutionary but massively flawed revision of its approach to sentencing criminal defendants. Driven by concerns of disparate treatment and undue leniency in punishment, Congress created an independent agency, the U.S. Sentencing Commission, to formulate a new sentencing regime that would drastically limit the discretion of federal judges. The resulting body of law, known as the Sentencing Guidelines, has both perverted constitutional principles and produced grave injustices.

In promulgating detailed sentencing rules that bind federal courts and individual parties, the commission is making law through an unconstitutional delegation of legislative authority. This practice not only violates the constitutional principle of separation of powers, but also severs the typical lines of political accountability in American democracy. Moreover, the Guidelines themselves violate a number of constitutional rights by, among other things, punishing defendants for uncharged or acquitted conduct.

Beyond constitutional infirmities, the Guidelines have proven to be unfair and unworkable in practice. Justice in sentencing requires an individualized assessment of the offender and the offense, leading to a moral judgment imposed by judges with skill, experience, and wisdom. Those judgments cannot be made by a distant bureaucracy pursuant to abstract rules that disregard important context. Yet that is precisely what occurs in today's federal courts: Individuals are sentenced under the commission's micro-managed rules, which expressly forbid judges from considering personal characteristics like the defendant's age and family responsibilities. That rigidity in sentencing has led to intentional deception among judges, prosecutors, and defense attorneys attempting to avoid the prescribed consequences of the Guidelines. Such dishonesty is flatly inconsistent with the commission's stated goal of "truth in sentencing."

Background

November 1, 2002, marks the 15th anniversary of the U.S. Sentencing Guidelines. But there will be no celebrations, parades, or other festivities in honor of the punishment scheme created by Congress and the U.S. Sentencing Commission. Instead, the day will pass like most others during the intervening decade and a half—with scores of federal defendants sentenced under a convoluted, hypertechnical, and mechanical system that saps moral judgment from the process of punishment. Rather than fanfare, the Guidelines' anniversary will likely be met with a level of ridicule reserved for [in the words of author Michael Tonry,] "the most disliked sentencing reform initiative in the United States in this century."

The Guidelines refer to the legal framework of rules for sentencing convicted federal offenders. After a defendant has been investigated by law enforcement, indicted by grand jury, and found guilty at trial (or through a plea bargain), the trial judge must determine an appropriate punishment under the Guidelines. Depending on the crime of conviction and various factors related to the offender and the offense, a federal judge will typically sentence the convicted defendant to a term of imprisonment and possibly a criminal fine. Of course, the federal system is dwarfed by the combined criminal justice systems of the individual states, the primary crime fighters in

American society. Of the nearly 2 million inmates in the United States, less than 10 percent are presently serving federal sentences.

Nonetheless, the federal system remains influential in the national debate on crime and punishment, presenting a prominent model for other jurisdictions in their penological experimentation. For better or worse, federal law enforcement continues to dominate certain categories of crime—such as drug offenses, immigration violations, and white-collar crime—often to the point of occupying the field. This tendency, particularly for narcotics offenses, has only increased since the enactment of the Sentencing Guidelines, resulting in a federal prison population that has quadrupled in just a decade and a half. In 1999, for example, more than 50,000 offenders were sentenced pursuant to the Guidelines, 44 percent of whom had been convicted of drug offenses.

Mandatory Minimums

Some commentators have tried to distinguish the Guidelines from another federal sentencing phenomenon: mandatory minimum sentences. Those punishment schemes set an absolute floor for sentencing particular offenders. In most cases, for instance, a conviction for possessing five grams of crack cocaine results in an automatic five-year sentence. In a 1991 report to Congress, the U.S. Sentencing Commission blasted mandatory minimums as, among other things, producing unwarranted disparities among offenders and transferring power from judges to prosecutors. The great irony, however, is that those same charges could be leveled against the commission's own work product. Like mandatory minimums, the Sentencing Guidelines set strict parameters for punishment (including a lower limit), absent some basis to depart from the sentencing range.

When Congress enacts a mandatory minimum, the relevant sentencing range shifts upward to meet the legislative mandate. Both the Guidelines and statutory minimums are manifestations of the same trend—mandatory or "determinate" sentencing. It is almost Orwellian doublespeak to call the present regime *guidelines*, given that judges must follow these sentencing rules or face reversal by appellate courts. In fact, the commission has even made the "Freudian slip" of calling the Guidelines "mandatory." Both mandatory minimums and the guidelines attempt to purge sentencing discretion in federal trial courts, all but precluding judges from departing from the strictures of determinate punishment. Far from being alternatives, these two schemes feed off each other in curbing judicial discretion. For that reason, both the Sentencing Guidelines and mandatory minimums will be collectively referred to in this study as the "Guidelines."

Guidelines a Failure

Although the Guidelines are frowned upon from all corners of the criminal justice system, the federal judiciary has been particularly adamant in its opposition to the current sentencing regime. Federal judges have described the Guidelines as "a dismal failure," "a farce," and "out of whack;" "a dark, sinister, and cynical crime management program" with "a certain Kafkaesque aura about it;" and "the greatest travesty of justice in our legal system in this century." In 1990, the Federal Courts Study Committee received testimony from 270 witnesses—including judges, prosecutors, defense attorneys, probation officers, and federal officials—and only four people expressed support for the Guidelines: the U.S. Attorney General and three members of the U.S. Sentencing Commission. Surveys of the judiciary have confirmed widespread disapproval of the Guidelines: A 1992 poll found that more than half of all federal judges believe that the current system should be completely eliminated, while a 1997 survey concluded that more than two-thirds of federal judges view the Guidelines as unnecessary.

With 15 years of overwhelmingly negative reaction, it is time to reconsider the Guidelines and the consequences for federal criminal justice. . . .

Abuses of the System

Kemba Smith—formerly federal inmate No. 26370-083, serving a 24-year sentence under the Guidelines—recently graduated from Virginia Union University with a 3.1 grade point average. Since her release from prison, Smith has reconnected with her now seven-year-old son, completed her bachelor's degree, worked part-time as a legal assistant and social work intern, and recounted her story at public forums and college campuses, warning other young people about the dangers of drugs and drug dealers. She has now set her sights on becoming a lawyer. "It just seems right for me to pursue law," Smith says, "to have that title to go along with my advocacy." After six years in prison, she is now ready to follow her dreams and provide for her family.

But neither the Guidelines nor the commission set Smith free; no judge or prosecutor was able to undo the draconian sentence that had been levied against this first-time, low-level offender. Instead, the 30-year-old mother, who had been caught in an abusive relationship with a drug kingpin, received mercy from a most unlikely source. At the end of his term, President Bill Clinton included Smith on a much ridiculed list of offenders who received executive pardons. Yet Smith's case is the exception proving the rule—the futility of trying to remedy excesses and injustices under the Guidelines without also changing the current sentencing system itself. Only a tiny fraction of pardon applications actually receive substantive review and an even smaller amount are granted by the president. The number is likely to dwindle even further under the [George W.] Bush administration, with the pardon fiasco of fugitive financier Marc Rich still fresh in the mind of the electorate.

More importantly, an infrequently used, postconviction approach cannot even start to ameliorate the harsh punishment demanded by the Guidelines. As suggested by the head of the NAACP's criminal justice project, "Kemba is . . . just the tip of the iceberg." Clarence Aaron and Dale Yirkovsky will remain in federal lock-up, as will countless other low level and first-time offenders who received cruel sentences under the Guidelines. They were punished not by the respective trial courts, but by a dehumanizing process that prevents moral judgment. Absent a repeal of the Guidelines, many more defendants will follow them into prison, fodder for the thoughtless machine that is federal sentencing.

Guidelines Should Be Scrapped

American conceptions of justice demand that the Guidelines be scrapped and the commission disbanded. Congress created an unconstitutional "fourth branch" of government, with the commission assuming the power to make law but lacking any type of political accountability. Moreover, the commission has usurped much of the judiciary's traditional authority over sentencing through its enactment of mandatory Guidelines that all but eliminate the capacity of trial courts to mete out individualized punishment. In turn, the current system has drastically expanded the power of federal prosecutors, giving them yet another tool with which to squeeze out information and guilty pleas from defendants while encouraging law enforcement to play fast-and-loose with the rules of evidence.

The Guidelines have also undermined the legitimacy of sentencing law, diluting and obscuring moral judgment. The complexity of the current system generates confusion among both criminal justice actors and lay citizens, while the hypertechnical character of the Guidelines produces sentencing variations that are nearly impossible to justify. The Guidelines also dehumanize the process of punishment by deeming relevant only certain factors about the offense or offender and

Power Grab

Rather than allowing judges to use their intrinsic judicial power of discretion to impose criminal sentences, mandatory minimums have been a power grab by both the legislative and executive branches. First, the legislative branch dictated one-size-fits-all sentences that courts must follow. Second, the executive, in the person of the prosecutor, influences the sentence because prosecutors have discretion to choose certain charges on the basis of the penalties they carry.

For all of these reasons, there has been steadily growing criticism of mandatory minimums by former prosecutors, federal judges, and other commentators and organizations.

Molly M. Gill,
Families Against Mandatory Minimums,
September 2008.

ignoring all others, mechanically plugging into the sentencing equation those privileged characteristics and then spitting out the bottom line of punishment.

Avoiding the Guidelines

To temper the severity of federal sentencing, prosecutors, defense attorneys, and even judges have engaged in the hidden nullification of the Guidelines, tinkering with case facts, for instance, in order to reach an agreeable sentence. Although this nullification may lead to just outcomes in particular cases, the process of fact bargaining engages the parties in blatant dishonesty, unbecoming to officers of the court. This corruption not only subverts the moral authority of the federal system, but also conflicts with the democratic prerequisites of open and accountable government. As a result, many practitioners, jurists, and even average citizens have come to view the Guidelines with cynicism and contempt.

There are many possible paths to positive change, all leading to the dissolution of the commission and the repeal of its Guidelines. Brave members of Congress might step up to the plate of their own accord, recognizing the injustice of the current system and instigating a new era of sentencing reform. A blue-ribbon commission, representing all parties with a stake in federal sentencing, could be impaneled and empowered to design an approach to punishment that avoids the Guidelines' many vices. It even seems possible that the citizenry itself might grow weary of the enormous financial and human costs, placing pressure on Congress to scrap the Guidelines and start again. But, however prompted, the American public and its elected officials will eventually have to face a fundamental choice: Is the sentencing process one of man or machine? In a recent speech, Judge Bruce Jenkins compared federal sentencing to speaking with a computer chip:

> We forget that the computer is just a tool. It is supposed to help, not substitute for thought. It is completely indifferent to compassion. It has no moral sense. It has no sense of fairness. It can add up figures, but can't evaluate the assumptions for which the figures stand. Its judgment is no judgment at all. There is no algorithm for human judgment.

In the end, the American people must decide whether defendants should be sentenced by the complex, hypertechnical rules of a mechanical process—or, instead, by an entity capable of individualized decisions made pursuant to wisdom and experience. If the last 15 years have proven anything it is that justice in sentencing cannot be served by the convoluted rules of a distant bureaucracy. Only trial judges can mete out punishment that fits both the offense and the offender, mindful of the deeply held notion that people must be treated as unique beings worthy of individualized treatment and not as undifferentiated objects on the conveyor belt of sentencing. Ultimately, Congress must end the Guidelines era and begin anew, guaranteeing that the next 15 years of federal punishment will not be like the last. It is time to scrap the commission and its Guidelines, and to embark on a new age of moral judgment in sentencing.

"Arizona's high incarceration rate is driven by a rigid mandatory sentencing system that ... crowds prisons with non-violent substance abusers."

Mandatory Minimum Sentences Result in Prison Overcrowding

Judith Greene and Kevin Pranis

Judith Greene is a research associate for Families Against Mandatory Minimums (FAMM) and Kevin Pranis is a criminal justice policy analyst for Justice Strategies. In the following report on Arizona's prison crisis, they show that Arizona's prison system is overcrowded with nonviolent offenders convicted of low-level crimes but sentenced to long stints in prison because of mandatory minimum sentencing laws. Greene and Pranis insist that most of these individuals are substance abusers who should be in drug treatment centers or other community-based programs rather than prison.

As you read, consider the following questions:

1. What do the authors say drives Arizona's high incarceration rate?

Judith Greene and Kevin Pranis, *Arizona Prison Crisis*, Washington, DC: Families Against Mandatory Minimums, 2004. Reproduced by permission.

2. According to Greene and Pranis, Arizona will need to add how many prison beds and increase its corrections budget by how much every year to keep pace with the current rate of growth?
3. What nonviolent offenses are fueling nearly half the growth in Arizona's prison population, according to the authors?

Arizona has become the incarceration capital of the western United States. With the ninth highest rate of incarceration in the nation, Arizona stands in stark contrast to neighboring states. The rate of prison population growth in 2002 was twice the regional average and the state incarcerates women, Latinos and African Americans at higher rates than its neighbors.

Arizona's high incarceration rate is driven by a rigid mandatory sentencing system that severely restricts judges' discretion in imposing sentences and crowds prisons with nonviolent substance abusers. Mandatory and lengthy "enhanced" prison terms are required for a variety of offenses, regardless of the facts in the case or the relative seriousness of the underlying conduct.

Except in cases involving first-time defendants charged with low-level property or drug offenses, the system places all sentencing discretion in the hands of prosecutors who decide what charges to file, whether to seek mandatory sentencing enhancements, whether to offer a plea, what concessions to offer, and whether a particular sentence will be required.

Too Many Prisoners

If incarceration were the magic bullet that tough-on-crime advocates claim, Arizona's reliance on imprisonment might be justified on crime-control grounds. Yet the state has the highest index crime rate in the nation and lags behind both neighboring states and the nation as a whole in crime reduction.

While doing little to reduce crime, mandatory sentencing laws and rapid prison expansion have imposed tremendous fiscal and human costs. The current level of corrections spending is inadequate to meet even the costs associated with the current prison population and is straining the state's ability to meet other critical needs.

For example, Arizona ranks 49th among 50 states in per pupil spending for kindergarten to 12th-grade education, while state universities doubled tuition to make up for steep budget cuts in 2003. Adequate funds are unavailable for drug courts, substance abuse and mental health treatment and other programs that increase public safety while reducing the need for prison beds.

New permanent prison beds authorized by the legislature are projected to increase annual prison operating costs by over $60 million. Yet the 3,400 new beds will cover just a *quarter* of the 13,584-bed deficit projected for fiscal year 2008. Arizona would need to add 2,000 beds and increase the corrections budget by nearly $40 million *every year* just to keep pace with the current rate of growth. . . .

Targeting Low-Level Offenders

Under Arizona's mandatory sentencing system, non-violent offenders make up the majority of state prisoners. One in four are serving time for a property offense, one in five for a drug offense and one in 12 for driving under the influence (DUI). The majority of non-violent offenders are serving time for low-level offenses. A handful of non-violent offenses—including DUI, forgery, fraud and theft—are fueling nearly half the growth in the prison population.

The large number of low-level and non-violent offenders behind bars is a product of Arizona's mandatory sentencing laws, which force judges to lock up individuals who commit repeat but petty offenses. Most of these individuals are substance abusers whose crimes are related to addiction and many

Incarceration Rates, per 100,000 Residents, for Sentenced Prisoners in 2002

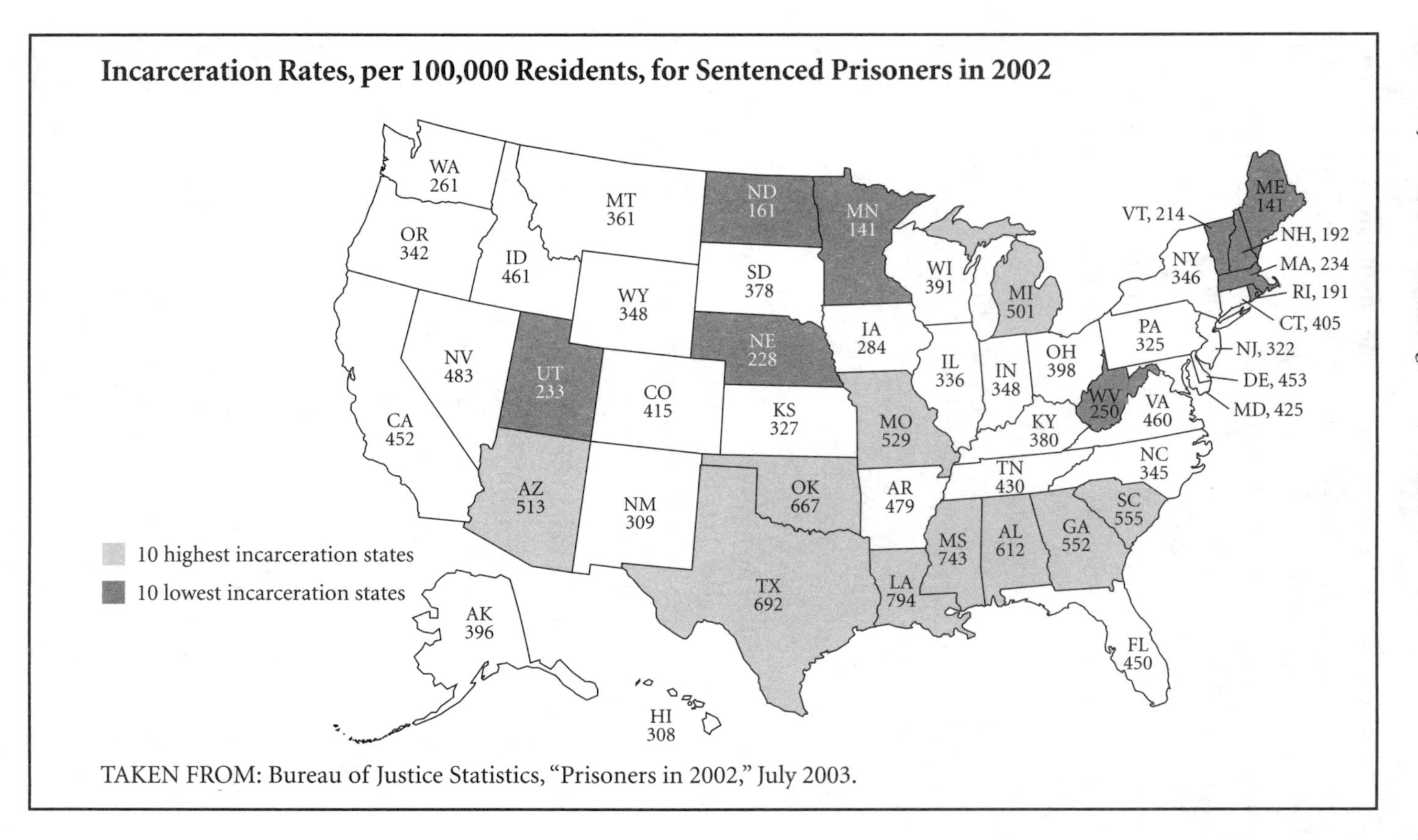

TAKEN FROM: Bureau of Justice Statistics, "Prisoners in 2002," July 2003.

should be in mandatory treatment and other community-based programs rather than prison.

When applied to non-dangerous offenses, Arizona's sentencing enhancements make little or no distinction between serious and petty offenders. For example, under the repetitive enhancement, an addict with one prior conviction for drug possession caught selling a gram of cocaine faces a sentence that is almost double that of a dealer caught with a kilo of cocaine for the first time.

Such an outcome flies in the face of common sense and the will of voters, who clearly intended that convictions for drug possession should *not* result in long prison terms. Yet if the enhancement is invoked and the prosecutor can prove the facts, the judge *must* impose an enhanced sentence.

The law prevents judges from imposing mandatory treatment and community-based sanctions on thousands of low-level non-violent offenders, even though these sentences would cost less, reduce recidivism and increase public safety more effectively than prison.

Against Common Sense

The result is long sentences for non-violent and often low-level offenses. For example, the majority of those admitted to prison for DUI are serving average terms of over three years. Those sentenced to prison for drug possession receive prison sentences of three-and-a-half years on average. And non-violent offenders sentenced with the repeat offender enhancement serve average prison terms longer than those imposed on most violent offenders.

Arizona's "truth-in-sentencing" statute mandating that prisoners serve at least 85 percent of their sentences also appears to weigh most heavily on non-violent offenders. Since the law was implemented in 1994, the average time served for non-violent offenses has increased far faster than the time served by violent and other serious person offenders.

Finally, laws that put the greatest number of non-violent offenders behind bars and account for the greatest growth in the prison population are written in such a way that serious charges can easily be brought against low-level offenders. For example, Arizona's drug laws treat the lowest-level sellers, most of whom are addicts, like drug "kingpins." Because virtually all drug sale offenses, including possession with intent to sell, are given the most serious felony designation aside from murder, addict-sellers can get prison terms longer than most violent offenders.

Rigidity in Sentencing

Where judges have discretion, in sentencing individuals revoked from probation, they help correct the imbalance by imposing the minimum available sentences on low-level sellers. But where prison sentences are set by plea bargains, addict-sellers can get prison terms longer than most violent offenders. As a result, the average sentence for drug sales is longer than the average sentence for assault or weapons charges.

Similarly, forgery and fraud statutes can be used to bring serious charges against petty offenders.

Forgery and fraud are leading contributors to growth in Arizona's prison population (especially for women) and now account for over a quarter (29.1 percent) of incarcerated property offenders. Unlike theft offenses, charges of forgery, fraud and trafficking in stolen property are not scaled according to monetary value and therefore can be used to bring serious charges against low-level offenders.

Within Arizona, there are sharp disparities in how different jurisdictions use costly prison beds—differences that do not correlate with crime rates. While the courts in most Arizona counties tend to lock up person offenders at similar rates, sentencing patterns vary widely in the use of incarceration for non-violent offenders. Thousands of prison beds could be saved by bringing incarceration rates for non-violent offenders sentenced in Maricopa County and a handful of rural counties in line with the rest of the state.

Pima County locks up violent offenders at higher rates than any other jurisdiction, yet the county's overall incarceration rate falls below the state average because the county targets prison beds to offenders who pose a real danger to the public.

Prison Instead of Treatment

Proposition 200 diverts hundreds convicted of first- and second-time drug possession from prison to treatment and saves taxpayers over $6 million a year. But because the measure applies only to personal drug possession and not low-level drug sales or other drug-related crime, Arizona continues to lock up thousands of non-violent offenders whose substance abuse, from a crime control perspective, would be better addressed by treatment in the community.

Department of Corrections (DOC) data show that non-violent substance abusers make up half of all prisoners and that the overwhelming majority of prisoners have chemical dependencies. Non-violent offenders are more likely to have severe substance abuse problems than violent offenders.

Arizona already has in place cost-effective, community-based programs that could do *more* than incarcerate to prevent further criminal behavior, but mandatory sentencing laws and a lack of funding prevent them from meeting the need. The state's drug courts, well regarded by criminal justice professionals, enroll just 764 offenders while the state incarcerates over 10,000 non-violent offenders with severe chemical dependencies. A re-entry program for drug offenders established in 2003 has room for just 200 participants although 4,800 could be eligible.

Women are the fastest-growing segment of the prison population yet also commit the least serious offenses by any measure. The number of women behind bars grew 58 percent between 1998 and 2003 and will have doubled by 2008 according to DOC projections. Three-fourths of incarcerated women are serving time for non-violent offenses and over half for low-level offenses.

Women prisoners are far more likely to suffer from chemical dependency and mental illness than their male counterparts. Three-fourths of women prisoners are assigned the highest possible alcohol and drug needs score, over half are methamphetamine users and one-quarter have serious mental health problems.

Arizona incarcerates African Americans and Latinos at higher rates than any neighboring state and both groups make up a significantly greater proportion of the prison population than the state population. Although two-thirds of Arizona residents are white, the majority of prisoners are people of color.

The overrepresentation of minorities in prison is particularly pronounced among drug and DUI offenders, with whites comprising just over a third that group. Analysis of leading drug and DUI offenses shows that African Americans and Latinos who are U.S. citizens consistently received longer prison terms than whites with similar prior felony records.

While further research is needed to pinpoint the causes of racial and ethnic disparity in the makeup of Arizona's prison population, these highly disturbing patterns suggest that in Arizona, as elsewhere, communities of color are disproportionately impacted by drug law enforcement.

Smart-on-Crime Strategies

As Arizona considers spending hundreds of millions to expand costly prisons, other states are moving toward smarter, less expensive sentencing and correctional strategies. Since the beginning of the fiscal crisis that has affected most states, policymakers—both Republicans and Democrats—in more than half of the states have introduced major reforms to improve the effectiveness of their sentencing and correctional systems, significantly reducing costs.

At least 18 states rolled back mandatory minimum sentences or restructured other harsh penalties enacted in preceding years to "get tough" on low-level drug offenders or non-violent lawbreakers. Legislators in 15 states have eased prison population pressures with mechanisms to shorten time served in prison, increase the release rate and handle those who violate release conditions without returning them to prison.

Michigan legislators repealed almost all mandatory minimum drug statutes—long cited as among the toughest in the nation—replacing them with drug sentencing guidelines that give discretion back to Michigan judges and the state expected a savings of $41 million in 2003 alone. Washington legislators enacted a package of reforms that give judges more discretion to divert non-violent drug offenders to treatment, reduce prison sentences for drug trafficking and increase early-release eligibility. As a result, the state expects to save an estimated $40 million over the next two years, and spend an additional $8 million on drug treatment.

There is broad public support for the move toward "smart-on-crime" strategies that emphasize prevention and treatment over incarceration for non-violent offenders. Recent national research on preferences about crime and corrections indicates strong support—by a two-to-one margin—for measures that address the causes of crime over strict sentencing. An October 2003 poll of Arizona registered voters found that Arizonans strongly support increased spending for child protective services but oppose a major expansion of the prison system.

Arizona's state system of adult probation is considered highly effective and a national model for ensuring public safety and holding offenders accountable in a community setting. Yet probation is not an option for many thousands of non-violent offenders under Arizona's mandatory sentencing system.

Periodical Bibliography

The following articles have been selected to supplement the diverse views presented in this chapter.

Sasha Abramsky	"The Dope Dealer Who Got 55 Years," *Progressive*, June 2006.
Robert Barnes	"Court Revisits Sentencing Guidelines," *Washington Post*, October 3, 2007.
Economist	"No More Room, No More Money," May 21, 2009.
Brian Gilmore	"Growth of Prison Population Reveals Moral Failure," *Progressive*, December 5, 2006.
Los Angeles Times	"Crack Cocaine and American Injustice," August 1, 2009.
Anthony Papa	"Gov. David Paterson Does the Right Thing," *Counterpunch*, May 11, 2009.
John Perazzo	"Obama: Tilting at Racial Windmills," *FrontPage Magazine*, December 16, 2008.
Larry Schwartztol	"Rocks and Powder," *Slate*, August 23, 2006.
Kemba Smith	"The Wisdom of Pardons," *USA Today*, December 17, 2008.
Eric E. Sterling and Julie Stewart	"Undo This Legacy of Len Bias's Death," *Washington Post*, June 24, 2006.
Jacob Sullum	"Crackbrained Crack Crackdown," *Reason*, May 23, 2007.
Katrina Vanden Heuvel	"We're Number 1!" *Nation*, April 23, 2008.
Washington Post	"Cocaine Justice," July 26, 2009.
James Q. Wilson	"Do the Time, Lower the Crime," *Los Angeles Times*, March 30, 2008.

Chapter 4

What Are Some Alternatives to Mandatory Minimum Sentencing?

Chapter Preface

As criticism of mandatory minimum sentences—especially three-strikes laws and mandatory drug sentences—has increased over the past several years, criminal justice and correctional experts have looked to find viable alternatives. Many critics advocate for the repeal of mandatory minimums, arguing that they are inherently unjust laws that penalize minorities and women and result in prison overcrowding in the regions that they are implemented. Others recommend broadening the "safety valve" provision that Congress passed in 1994 to address the harsh sentences served by nonviolent drug offenders. For example, if a judge finds that a defendant is a low-level, nonviolent, first-time offender who qualifies for the provision, the defendant may be sentenced under the sentencing guidelines instead of the mandatory minimum sentencing law. Although many observers feel that the safety valve is a step in the right direction, they also point out that the criteria for eligibility are very narrow; as a result, thousands of nonviolent drug defendants are still sent to prison for decades under mandatory minimum sentencing laws.

For offenders convicted of drug offenses eligible for mandatory minimum sentences, many experts have turned to the drug court system to provide punishment and rehabilitation. A drug court allows the judge, the district attorney, public defender or private defense attorney, drug treatment counselor, and probation officer to work together in a nonadversarial fashion to help drug-addicted offenders obtain the necessary treatment and rehabilitation they must have to break their cycle of crime and addiction. Offenders appear frequently before the judge at status hearings in the drug court while undergoing substance abuse treatment and have other supervisory constraints (including drug testing) for at least one year. Supporters contend that drug courts allow the criminal justice system to work cooperatively with treatment systems and others to provide convicted criminals with the much-needed tools to get into recovery, stay in recovery, and lead a productive, crime-free life.

Critics of drug courts as an alternative sentencing option argue that there is little evidence to believe that they show sustained benefits both in terms of drug usage and recidivism. They cite studies to show that a significant percentage of offenders enrolled in drug courts drop out of court-mandated treatment programs and therefore fail out of drug court. These critics contend the increasing popularity of drug courts are essentially a waste of time and resources.

The viewpoints in the following chapter debate the long-term efficacy of drug courts as a viable alternative to mandatory minimum sentences and discuss broadening the "safety valve" provision, drug treatment programs, and repealing mandatory minimum sentences altogether.

VIEWPOINT 1

"No other justice intervention can rival the results produced by drug courts."

Drug Court Supervision Is a Viable Alternative to Mandatory Minimum Sentences

C. West Huddleston III, Douglas B. Marlowe, and Rachel Casebolt

C. West Huddleston III, is the chief executive officer of the National Association of Drug Court Professionals (NADCP) and executive officer of the National Drug Court Institute (NDCI). Douglas B. Marlowe is the chief of research, law, and policy at NADCP, and Rachel Casebolt is a research coordinator for NDCI. In the following viewpoint, they advocate the effectiveness of drug courts in breaking the cycle of substance abuse, addiction, and crime and propose drug courts as a viable alternative to throwing low-level, nonviolent drug offenders in jail because of harsh mandatory minimum sentences.

C. West Huddleston III, Douglas B. Marlowe, and Rachel Casebolt, "Painting the Current Picture: A National Report on Drug Courts and Other Problem-Solving Court Programs in the United States," *National Drug Court Institute*, May 2008.

As you read, consider the following questions:

1. How many adult drug courts were in the United States in 2007, according to the authors?
2. According to the authors, how many adult drug courts have a probationary or post-plea condition?
3. According to research conducted by the Treatment Research Institute and cited by the Huddleston, Marlowe, and Casebolt, drug court is especially effective for what kind of offender?

Drug courts represent the coordinated efforts of justice and treatment professionals to actively intervene and break the cycle of substance abuse, addiction, and crime. As an alternative to less effective interventions, drug courts quickly identify substance-abusing offenders and place them under ongoing judicial monitoring and community supervision, coupled with effective, long-term treatment services.

In this blending of systems, the drug court participant undergoes an intensive regimen of substance abuse treatment, case management, drug testing, and probation supervision while reporting to regularly scheduled status hearings before a judge with specialized expertise in the drug court model. In addition, drug courts increase the probability of participants' success by providing a wide array of ancillary services such as mental health treatment, trauma and family therapy, job skills training, and many other life-skill enhancement services.

Research verifies that no other justice intervention can rival the results produced by drug courts. Drug courts are demonstratively effective. According to over a decade of research, drug courts significantly improve substance abuse treatment outcomes, substantially reduce crime, and produce greater cost benefits than any other justice strategy. Scientists from the Treatment Research Institute at the University of Pennsylvania reported in 2003, "To put it bluntly, we know

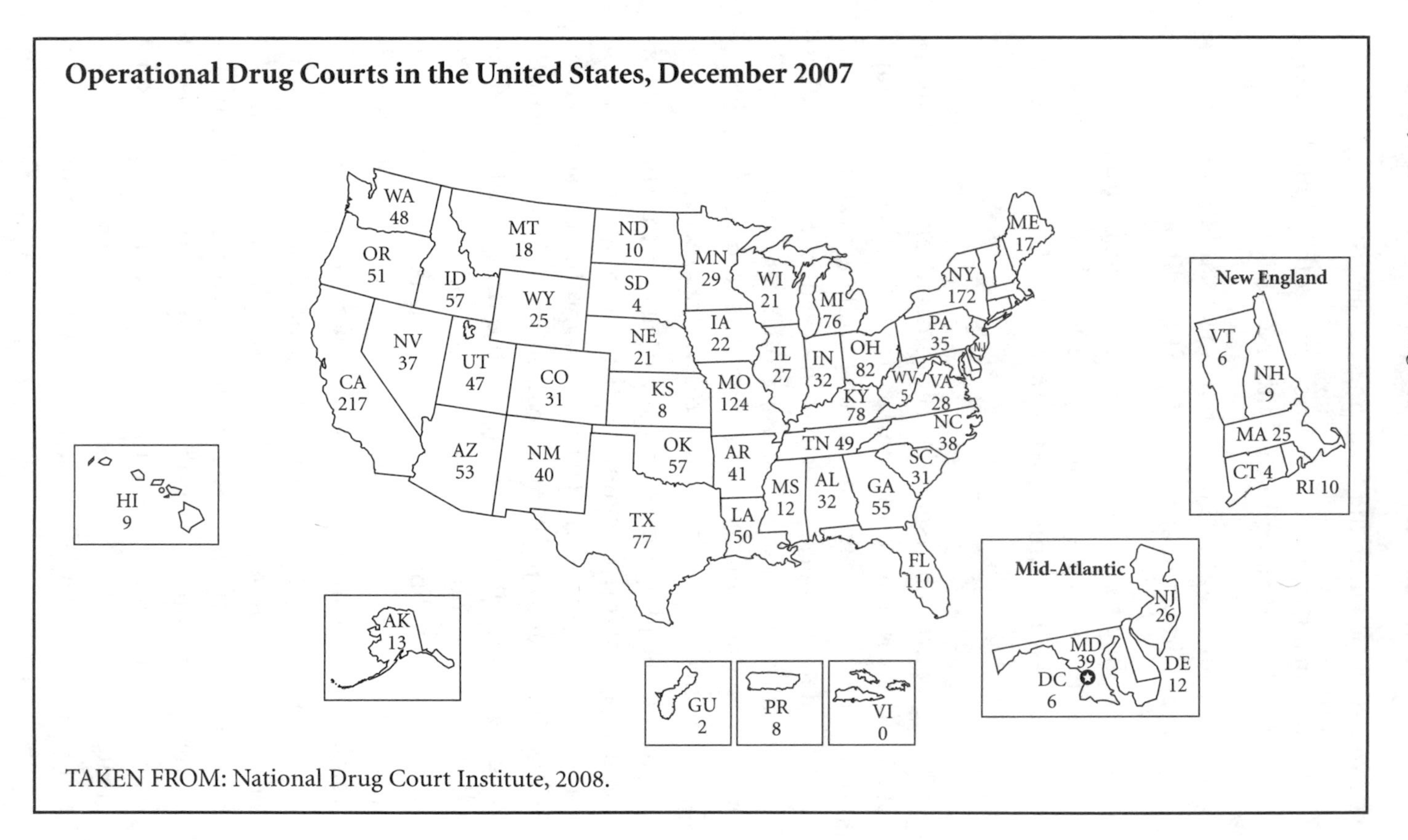

Operational Drug Courts in the United States, December 2007
WA 48
OR 51
CA 217
ID 57
NV 37
MT 18
WY 25
UT 47
AZ 53
CO 31
NM 40
ND 10
SD 4
NE 21
KS 8
OK 57
TX 77
MN 29
IA 22
MO 124
AR 41
LA 50
WI 21
IL 27
MS 12
MI 76
IN 32
KY 78
TN 49
AL 32
OH 82
WV 5
GA 55
FL 110
PA 35
VA 28
NC 38
SC 31
NY 172
ME 17
New England
VT 6
NH 9
MA 25
CT 4
RI 10
Mid-Atlantic
NJ 26
MD 39
DC 6
DE 12
HI 9
AK 13
GU 2
PR 8
VI 0
TAKEN FROM: National Drug Court Institute, 2008.

that drug courts outperform virtually all other strategies that have been used with drug-involved offenders." Additionally, Columbia University's historic analysis of drug courts concluded that drug courts provide "closer, more comprehensive supervision and much more frequent drug testing and monitoring during the program than other forms of community supervision. More importantly, drug use and criminal behavior are substantially reduced while offenders are participating in drug court." In 2005, the U.S. Government Accountability Office (GAO) published an extensive review of drug court research and concluded that adult drug court programs substantially reduce crime by lowering re-arrest and conviction rates among drug court graduates well after program completion, and thus, greater cost/benefits for drug court participants and graduates than comparison group members.

Why Drug Courts Work

As of December 31, 2007, there are 2,147 drug courts in operation, a 32% increase from 2004. Drug courts are an exemplar of best practices with substance-involved offenders. Treatment is not enough—immediacy and certainty of responses are critical for behavioral change, and judicial intervention and oversight are the best ways to implement best practices and elicit exceptional outcomes.

Ultimately, the power of drug court lies in improving lives and saving families. Drug courts give hope to the hopeless by reuniting parents with children, citizens with their community, and spouses with one another. As one drug court judge sums up the immeasurable impact of drug court:

> I was sitting at our November Graduation last week. I saw a woman who I remember from her first drug court session two years ago. At that time, she was physically anxious, her face was gaunt, shaking, crying uncontrollably, and had [been] about a week off of meth. She couldn't even sign the attendance sheet. She was insane and appeared delusional as

> she cried to the group about how her husband had left, that she had no place to stay, that meth had destroyed her, and that she didn't think she could make it in the program. All she needed was a chance.
>
> As she made her graduation speech to a full courtroom of participants, family, and friends, it seemed there was an entirely different individual before the court and her peers. Her face was glowing, she had celebrated 2 years of sobriety, and her 15 year old son stood up and addressed the court in tears that he was grateful the drug court program had given his mother back to him. There was not a dry eye in the court room. I had chills from being able to be a part of the miracle of recovery. It is one of the most powerful experiences I ever observed. The most rewarding part of my job is being able to see and be a part of those who work a program of recovery. Drug court works miracles!

Success Speaks for Itself

Drug courts offer a light in the midst of the darkness. From the Texas architect who did not lose his professional license because drug court, while facilitating his sobriety, spared him a felony conviction, to the California mother who, as a drug court graduate, inspired her alcoholic father to seek recovery after 40 years of addiction, the personal accounts of drug court's effectiveness are impressive.

Headlines across the nation offer tales of success born of drug courts: "Courting Addiction: Drug Court Gives Addicted Felons One Last Chance"; "Drug Court Proves It's Worth Effort: Offenders Must Give Back to Community"; "Where Miracles Can Happen: The Promise of Drug Court Programs"; "Holistic Court Gives a Teen Hope for a Drug-Free Future".

An *Oklahoma Gazette* article simply titled "Antidote" speaks of drug court's impact on a young woman named Stephanie.

> Arrested at 3 o'clock in the morning, driving with her husband in a car full of stolen property, bad credit cards and

> drugs, she had been doing methamphetamine for seven hard years with two prior felony convictions. The drug habit drove her crimes; she needed money for her next fix. She would be put in prison for 28 years to life on one more conviction.
>
> But, instead, two and a half years later, she's drug free, holding a job at an Oklahoma City violin sales business and helping others who are facing the same dark future she avoided ... In [her] experience, drug court is a necessity. Someone hooked on drugs, driven to commit crimes to support a habit, can't break the cycle alone, she said.

The life changes wrought by drug court are far more than cosmetic. For some, the changes are life saving. In a *Chico [CA] News & Review* article, Tricia N. acknowledged thoughts of suicide at the time she entered drug court. Tricia was introduced to drug court at a time when she had nothing more to lose. "I was out there on the streets ... and the drugs weren't working anymore. I didn't know where else to turn. I didn't want to be here anymore, [I] just wanted to check out." Less than 2 years later, a clean and sober, gainfully employed, eight-months pregnant, and soon to be married Tricia credits the drug court program for saving her life. She now works with other recovering addicts.

Success No Fluke

With the application of scientifically sound practices, drug court's effectiveness is no fluke. The melding of the criminal justice and therapeutic systems helps effectuate change from state to state in myriad individuals from all backgrounds.

Now numbering 1,174, adult drug courts comprise the majority of operational problem-solving court programs in the United States. Unlike the first generation of adult drug court programs, which tended to be diversionary or pre-plea models, today only 7% of adult drug courts are diversionary programs compared to 59% which are strictly post conviction.

Interestingly, another 19% of adult drug courts report serving both pre-adjudication and post-plea participants. In all, 915 or 78% of adult drug courts nationwide have a probationary or post-plea condition, suggesting that drug courts are working more often with a higher risk and higher need offender population.

This trend seems quite appropriate in light of research conducted by the Treatment Research Institute at the University of Pennsylvania, which concluded that high-risk clients who have more serious antisocial propensities or drug-use histories performed substantially better in drug court when they were required to attend frequent status hearings before the judge. Some of the most recent research on drug court reports their effects are greatest for "high-risk" offenders who have more severe criminal histories and drug problems. This suggests that drug courts may be best suited for the more incorrigible and drug-addicted offenders who cannot be safely or effectively managed in the community on standard probation.

Viewpoint 2

"It is time for the proponents of drug courts to 'come clean' with the numerous problems that plague the drug court initiative."

Drug Court Supervision Is Not a Realistic Alternative to Mandatory Minimum Sentences

Steven K. Erickson

Steven K. Erickson is the John M. Olin Fellow in Law at the University of Pennsylvania Law School. In the following viewpoint, he argues that there have been some serious questions about the efficacy of drug courts as an alternative to incarceration. He contends that drug courts are poor public policy.

As you read, consider the following questions:

1. How many drug courts were in operation in 2004, according to the author?
2. What does Erickson claim is the range for completion rates for many drug court studies?

Steven K. Erickson, "The Drug Court Fraud," Criminal Justice Legal Foundation, 2007. Reproduced by permission of the author.

3. According to the author, how do drug courts affect judges?

Drug courts are widely popular these days and have been heralded as a progressive system for dealing with chronic behaviors that often involve "revolving-door" defendants who cycle in and out of the criminal justice system. Indeed, state and federal governments have largely bought into this model of handling highly recidivistic crimes [those with repeat offenders]. In 2004, the GAO [Government Accountability Office] reported over 1,700 drug courts were in operation nationwide and a projected $69.86 million dollar budget for 2007. But there are serious questions about drug courts, both in terms of effectiveness and policy.

Drug Courts' Effectiveness

Numerous studies have praised drug courts for reducing participant recidivism and instilling sobriety. Yet many of these studies are fatally flawed from a methodological standpoint. These include: failure to use intent-to-treat analysis, inadequate or absent comparison groups, short follow-up periods, and sweeping conclusions.

Intent-to-treat analysis. It is not unreasonable to assume that most people would think that in evaluating whether drug courts work, evaluation studies would include those participants who drop out of the program before completion. Surely, it is not unfathomable to any attorney or mental health professional that many people who enter into drug treatment (especially unplanned, as is the case a drug arrest and subsequent diversion to drug court) will become dissatisfied and quit. However, most studies that have examined the "effectiveness" of drug courts have *not* included these participants. Only participants who completed the entire program are included in any analyses. From a methodological perspective, this is a fatal flaw. In statistics, we talk of "intent-to-treat analysis" which means that *all* people who are intended to receive the treatment are included in the final analysis—irrespective of whether they actually do. Virtually all medical and scientific studies *require* intent-to-treat analysis to avoid inflated estimates of effectiveness. Many of the drug court studies do not. Consequently, any claims made by these studies that drug courts are "effective" are highly dubious.

Comparison groups. Another fundamental property of any good research design examining an intervention strategy is the use of a valid comparison group. That is, you need to compare your intervention to something else so that you can correctly conclude that your intervention was likely associated with any observed events during the study (e.g., reduced arrests). Most drug court studies do not use comparison groups or use highly questionable methods in establishing a comparison group. For a comparison group to be valid, it must be *random*. That is, the chance of becoming a participant in drug court or traditional criminal court must not be influenced by external factors such as choice. Yet, many drug court studies allow only persons with "minor" criminal histories into drug court while allowing anyone into the comparator group. Thus, the comparisons are invalid since the groups are inherently unequal.

Short follow-up periods. It is well known in the addictions research literature that sobriety for 6 months or longer is necessary for long-term sobriety success. While there are several drug court studies that have followed participants for 6 months (and even 1 year), these studies have included the time when the participants are under the supervision of the court. Since the court holds leverage over the participants during this time (the courts can impose sanctions including jail time), any "success" during this period can theoretically be attributed to the heavy hand of the court and not necessarily the intervention itself. Since court supervision is not indefinite (nor should it be), the real question left unanswered is whether sobriety continues *beyond* drug court supervision.

Amount of Time to Elapse until Drug Court Judge Received Failed Drug-testing Results

	Percent
Minutes	18.8
One day	23.5
Two days	11.4
Three days	14.9
Four or more days	28.2
Missing	3.1
Total	100.0

TAKEN FROM: Bureau of Justice Assistance, 2003.

Sweeping conclusions. Proponents of drug courts often claim that numerous studies have conclusively demonstrated that drug courts work. Besides the numerous problems mentioned above, their own data simply does not support these sweeping conclusions. Completion rates for many drug court studies range from 25 to 66 percent. Thus, up to 2/3 of the initial participants *do not complete treatment*. If this is success, I'd hate to see what failure is. Moreover, success is often not well defined other than completion of the program. As mentioned before, the real question is whether drug courts have *sustained* benefits both in terms of drug usage and recidivism. This little evidence, if any, to believe that drug courts have accomplished either.

Public Policy

In his well-written article in the *North Carolina Law Review* in 2000, Judge Morris Hoffman lays out several cogent arguments why drug courts are bad public policy. Chief among these:

Diminution of counsel advocacy. By their very design, drug courts diminish the zealous advocacy role of defense counsel by encouraging a "treatment team" approach to drug offenders. Thus, rather than defending clients, defense attorneys are supposed to assist the court in coercing defendants into participation and reporting to the "team" whether the client has made progress on their sobriety. Besides the obvious dismissal of the attorney-client privilege, such approaches effectively eliminate the role of defense counsel as traditionally understood for centuries in American jurisprudence.

Judges as treatment leaders. Drug courts place judges at the forefront by having them actively engage in monitoring the treatment progress of participants. Drug court judges routinely hold meetings before scheduled appearances in which social workers, prosecutors, and defense counsel discuss a defendant's progress. Judges then make decisions as to how to "tweak" the treatment (e.g., more weekly contact with mental health). Yet judges are not mental health professionals; they are judges whose job is to oversee the proper administration of justice. Drug courts dispose of this well-established role in favor of a "jack of all trades" approach in which judges are transformed into quasi-mental health providers.

It is time for the proponents of drug courts to "come clean" with the numerous problems that plague the drug court initiative. As Judge Hoffman eloquently put it:

> We have succumbed to the lure of drug courts, to the lure of their federal dollars, to the lure of their hope, and to the lure of their popularity. Drug courts themselves have become a kind of institutional narcotic upon which the entire criminal justice system is becoming increasingly dependent.

Indeed, drug courts are not just a popular model for handling drug offenders, the principles of the drug court model have already been widely adapted in the emerging mental health court model whereby mentally ill offenders are diverted into specialty courts under the ruse of solving complex social problems through modified judicial institutions. The transformation of criminal justice under such a faulty model should trouble us all.

Viewpoint 3

"[The government should] amend [legislation] to broaden the safety valve."

The "Safety Valve" Provision Should Be Broadened

The Constitution Project

The Constitution Project is a nonprofit organization that aims to find viable solutions to a number of legal and constitutional problems. In the following viewpoint, the organization argues that the "safety valve" provision of mandatory minimum sentencing laws is too limited—it defines the low-level offender too narrowly, and therefore is not as effective as it could be. The Constitution Project recommends broadening the safety valve and making it available to all offenders who are subject to mandatory minimum sentences.

As you read, consider the following questions:

1. What does the author recognize as the two types of federal sentencing laws?
2. How does the Constitution Project define the safety valve provision in the viewpoint?

The Constitution Project, "Smart on Crime: Recommendations for the Next Administration and Congress," Washington, DC: The 2009 Criminal Justice Transition Coalition. Reproduced by permission.

3. What is the problem with the "tell-all" requirement, according to the author?

There are two types of federal sentencing laws: mandatory minimum sentencing laws, enacted by Congress, and the sentencing guidelines, promulgated by the United States Sentencing Commission and approved by Congress. A mandatory minimum sentence is a required minimum term of punishment (typically incarceration) that is established by Congress in a statute. When a mandatory minimum applies, the judge is forced to follow it and cannot impose a sentence below the minimum term required, regardless of the unique facts and circumstances of the defendant or the offense. Sentencing guidelines, in contrast, can be nuanced and crafted to account for both consistency in sentencing and individual circumstances of the offense and offender. Where both statutory mandatory minimums and guidelines apply, the mandatory minimum trumps the guidelines.

In the mid-1980s, Congress responded to public fears about the growing crack cocaine epidemic by adopting mandatory minimums of five and ten years to punish serious and high-level drug traffickers. In 1988, mandatory minimum penalties were extended to apply to conspirators as well as principals. Because the application of these mandatory minimums depended on one factor, drug weight, they could not be adjusted to account for factors such as playing a limited role in the offense. This had the unfortunate consequence of treating all participants in a drug scheme the same way, including very low-level drug couriers and assistants, who are subject to the same lengthy sentence as kingpins.

Safety Valve Provisions

In response to widespread criticism that mandatory minimums are unduly harsh in many circumstances, as they cannot meaningfully distinguish among defendants of different culpability, in 1994 Congress created a "safety valve" that would suspend the operation of the otherwise applicable mandatory minimum in drug cases if the defendant was a low-level participant, did not use a weapon, was involved in a violence-free crime, had little or no criminal history and told the government the truth about his or her involvement in the offense and offenses in the same course of conduct or common scheme or plan.

The statutory safety valve obliges courts to impose a sentence under the advisory guidelines in place of a mandatory minimum upon a judicial finding that the conditions of [the safety valve] are met. Today, the safety valve has been used to recognize and adjust the sentences of 25 percent of all drug offenders, benefiting first-time, low-level, nonviolent offenders. This means judges can craft sentences that more accurately punish offenders based on the severity of their offense, their culpability, and their criminal history.

The safety valve, while of great benefit, suffers from several problems that should be corrected. First, it defines low-level offenders much too narrowly, relying on the point system established by the Sentencing Commission for calculation of criminal history. Second, the "tell-all" requirement is confusing to judges, defense attorneys, and prosecutors and has been misinterpreted to require defendants to provide information about other offenders (not just themselves), which is covered by a separate statutory section. Third, there is no sound reason to limit the application of the safety valve, which seeks to recognize and fashion appropriate sentences for first time, low-level, nonviolent offenders who recognize and admit their responsibility, to only those defendants who were convicted of a drug offense.

Proposed Solutions

1. Amend [legislation] to broaden the safety valve.

Mandatory Minimums: Locking Up More Drug Offenders, Longer

Drug offenses are the largest single category of federal convictions:

- **34 percent** of all federal offenders in 2007 were sentenced for a drug offense.
- **67 percent** of all federal drug offenders received a mandatory minimum:
  - **28 percent** received a five-year mandatory minimum
  - **39 percent** received a minimum sentence of 10 years or more

Percentage of drug offenders receiving mandatory minimums:

- **82 percent** of crack cocaine offenders
- **81 percent** of methamphetamine offenders
- **79 percent** of powder cocaine offenders

Some benefit from the "safety valve":

- **25 percent** of federal drug offenders who would have been subject to a mandatory minimum received a shorter sentence under the 1994 "safety valve" provision available to non-violent, low-level, first-time drug offenders.

TAKEN FROM: United States Sentencing Commission, 2007 Annual Report.

To be eligible for the safety valve waiver of the mandatory minimum, a defendant must be found to satisfy five criteria. One of them concerns the extent of the offender's criminal history, which in turn relies on the point system established by the Sentencing Commission for calculation of criminal history. The intent of the safety valve was to allow courts to recognize offenders with no or limited criminal history. Due to the peculiarities of the sentencing guidelines' criminal history provisions, people who have been convicted of more than one very minor offense, such as driving on a suspended license or passing a bad check, can be considered to have too much criminal background to qualify for the safety valve. Changing the criteria slightly will permit the safety valve to assist some offenders whose criminal history points overstate their actual risk of recidivism. Congress can change the criminal history criteria by including defendants who fall into the Sentencing Commission's Criminal History Category I, whether due to the defendant's criminal history or due to a departure from a higher criminal history category that, in the court's opinion, overstates the actual criminal history of the defendant.

2. Amend [legislation] to substitute acceptance of responsibility for the tell-all requirement.

Congress can also improve the safety valve by replacing the tell-all requirement with a requirement that the defendant accept responsibility for the offense. The tell-all requirement is confusing to judges, defense attorneys, and prosecutors and has been interpreted to require defendants to provide information about other offenders, not just their own conduct. It has been a hotly litigated issue, as defense counsel and prosecutors argue about how much information is enough, whether it was provided in a timely fashion and how far beyond the offense of conviction a defendant must go in his or her submission. There is already a separate provision in criminal law that rewards cooperation with the prosecution with a reduction in sentence below the mandatory minimum when that cooperation substantially assists the government in an investigation or prosecution. Reductions for such "substantial assistance" are controlled by prosecutors pursuant to a guidelines provision requiring a government motion.

In lieu of the tell-all requirement, we would propose an acceptance of responsibility requirement. Acceptance of responsibility means that the defendant acknowledges his or her role in the offense early in the process, saving significant resources and eliminating the sometimes time- and resource-consuming process of determining whether or not a defendant has provided enough (or timely enough) information about his offense. Acceptance of responsibility standards are well established, as they have been a longstanding feature of the guidelines.

3. Amend [legislation] to expand the safety valve.

Federal mandatory minimum sentences have been added to a number of offenses, but the safety valve only applies to drug offenders. The problems associated with mandatory minimum drug sentences are replicated in other mandatory minimum-bearing offenses. There is no sound reason to limit the application of the safety valve, which seeks to recognize and fashion appropriate sentences for first time, low-level, non-violent offenders who recognize and admit their responsibility, to only those defendants convicted of drug offenses. Therefore, the safety valve should be made available for all offenses that are subject to mandatory minimums.

VIEWPOINT 4

"The ABA believes that . . . the . . . sentencing system would remain badly flawed as long as mandatory minimum sentences are prescribed by statute."

Mandatory Minimum Sentence Laws Should Be Repealed

James E. Felman

James E. Felman is an attorney in South Florida and cochair of the Criminal Justice Section Committee on Sentencing for the American Bar Association (ABA). In the following congressional testimony, he recommends that not only the crack-powder cocaine sentencing disparity be eliminated but that all mandatory sentences be repealed. Felman asserts that the ABA has recommended the "repeal of all mandatory minimum statutes and the expanded use of alternatives to incarceration for non-violent offenders."

As you read, consider the following questions:

1. The ABA has a membership of how many lawyers, according to Felman?

2. What percentage of those sentenced under federal crack cocaine laws are African Americans, according to the author?
3. According to Felman, what did Supreme Court Justice Anthony Kennedy say about mandatory minimum sentences?

The crack-powder [sentencing] disparity is simply wrong and the time to fix it is now. It has been more than a decade since the American Bar Association joined an ever-growing consensus of those involved in and concerned about criminal justice issues that the disparity in sentences for crack and powder cocaine offenses is unjustifiable and plainly unjust. We applaud this Subcommittee and its leadership for conducting this hearing as an important step in ending once and for all this enduring and glaring inequity.

The American Bar Association is the world's largest voluntary professional organization, with a membership of over 400,000 lawyers (including a broad cross-section of prosecuting attorneys and criminal defense counsel), judges and law students worldwide. The ABA continuously works to improve the American system of justice and to advance the rule of law in the world. I appear today at the request of ABA President William H. Neukom to reiterate to this Subcommittee the ABA's position on sentencing for cocaine offenses.

In 1995 the House of Delegates of the American Bar Association, after careful study, overwhelmingly approved a resolution endorsing the proposal submitted by the United States Sentencing Commission that would have resulted in crack and powder cocaine offenses being treated similarly and would have taken into account in sentencing aggravating factors such as weapons use, violence, or injury to another person. The American Bar Association has never wavered from the position that it took in 1995.

No Reason for Draconian Sentences

The Sentencing Commission's May 2002 *Report to the Congress: Cocaine and Federal Sentencing Policy* confirms the ABA's considered judgment that there are no arguments supporting the draconian [excessively harsh] sentencing of crack cocaine offenders as compared to powder cocaine offenders. The Sentencing Commission's 2002 *Report* provides an exhaustive accounting of the research, data, and viewpoints that led to the Commission's recommendations for crack sentencing reform. The recommendations include:

- Raising the crack cocaine quantities that trigger the five-year and ten-year mandatory minimum sentences in order to focus penalties on serious and major traffickers;
- Repeal of the mandatory minimum penalty for simple possession of crack cocaine; and
- Rejection of legislation that addresses the drug quantity disparity between crack and powder cocaine by lowering the powder cocaine quantities that trigger mandatory minimum sentences.

Unfortunately, the Sentencing Commission's 2002 recommendations were not addressed. Recognizing the enduring unfairness of current policy, the Sentencing Commission returned to the issue and recently took an important, although limited, first step toward addressing these issues by reducing crack offense penalties by two offense levels in its 2007 amendments to the Sentencing Guidelines. As the Sentencing Commission explained in its report accompanying the amendment, *Report to the Congress: Cocaine and Federal Sentencing Policy* (May 2007), the Commission felt its two-level adjustment was as far as it should go given its inability to alter Congressionally established mandatory minimum penalties and its recognition that establishing federal cocaine sentencing policy ulti-

A Flawed Policy

It is clear to the NACDL [National Association of Criminal Defense Lawyers], the United States Sentencing Commission, the Chief Justice of the United States Supreme Court, the American Bar Association and a greater portion of the public than Congress may recognize, that mandatory minimum sentencing policy is flawed throughout. It removes discretion from the judge, creates a uniform approach to sentencing that is unfair, reduces transparency in the criminal justice system, leads to racial and ethnically disparate sentencing, is not cost effective, does not reduce crime and has led to a prison population that will soon hit the two million mark. It is up to all of you to consider when our breaking point will be reached. By this I do not mean the time when, as a society, we cry enough. I do not mean this for such a cry has been heard for many years past as we have locked up our sons and daughters in the name of a war—a war on ourselves.

William B. Moffitt,
Testimony Before the House Subcommittee on Criminal Justice, Drug Policy, and Human Resources, May 11, 2000.

mately is Congress's prerogative. But it is critical to understand that this "minus-two" amendment is only a first step in addressing the inequities of the crack-powder disparity. The Sentencing Commission's 2007 *Report* made it plain that it views its recent amendment "only as a partial remedy" which is "neither a permanent nor a complete solution." As the Sentencing Commission noted, "[a]ny comprehensive solution requires appropriate legislative action by Congress."

Origins of Mandatory Sentences

The federal sentencing polices at issue in the 2002 and 2007 Sentencing Commission *Reports* were enacted in the Anti-Drug Abuse Act of 1986, which created a 100 to 1 quantity sentencing disparity between crack and powder cocaine, pharmacologically identical drugs. This means that crimes involving just five grams of crack, 10 to 50 doses, receive the same five-year mandatory minimum prison sentence as crimes involving 500 grams of powder cocaine, 2,500 to 5,000 doses. The 100-1 ratio yields sentences for crack offenses three to six times longer than those for powder offenses involving equal amounts of drugs. Many myths about crack were perpetuated in the late 1980s that claimed, for example, that crack cocaine caused violent behavior or that it was instantly addictive. Since then, research and extensive analysis by the Sentencing Commission has revealed that such assertions are not supported by sound evidence and, in retrospect, were exaggerated or simply false.

Although the myths perpetuated in the 1980s about crack cocaine have proven false, the disparate impact of this sentencing policy on the African American community continues to grow. The 1995 ABA policy, which supports treating crack and powder cocaine offenses similarly, was developed in recognition that the different treatment of these offenses has a "clearly discriminatory effect on minority defendants convicted of crack offenses." According to the 2007 *Report* by the Sentencing Commission, African Americans constituted 82% of those sentenced under federal crack cocaine laws. This is despite the fact that 66% of those who use crack cocaine are Caucasian or Hispanic. This prosecutorial disparity between crack and powder cocaine results in African Americans spending substantially more time in federal prisons for drug offenses than Caucasian offenders. Indeed, the Sentencing Commission reported that revising the crack cocaine threshold would do more to reduce the sentencing gap between African

Americans and Caucasians "than any other single policy change," and would "dramatically improve the fairness of the federal sentencing system." The ABA believes that it is imperative that Congress act quickly to finally correct the gross unfairness that has been the legacy of the 100 to 1 ratio....

ABA Opposes Mandatory Minimums

It is important that I emphasize, however, that the ABA not only opposes the crack-powder differential, but also strongly opposes the mandatory minimum sentences that are imposed for all cocaine offenses. The ABA believes that if the differential penalty structure is modified so that crack and powder offenses are dealt with in a similar manner, the resulting sentencing system would remain badly flawed as long as mandatory minimum sentences are prescribed by statute.

At its 2003 annual meeting, Supreme Court Justice Anthony Kennedy challenged the legal profession to begin a new public dialogue about American sentencing practices. He raised fundamental questions about the fairness and efficacy of a justice system that disproportionately imprisons minorities. Justice Kennedy specifically addressed mandatory minimum sentences and stated, "I can neither accept the necessity nor the wisdom of federal mandatory minimum sentences." He continued that "[i]n too many cases, mandatory minimum sentences are unwise or unjust."

The Kennedy Commission

In response to Justice Kennedy's concerns, the ABA established a Commission (the ABA Justice Kennedy Commission) to investigate the state of sentencing in the United States and to make recommendations on how to address the problems Justice Kennedy identified. One year to the day that Justice Kennedy addressed the ABA, the ABA House of Delegates approved a series of policy recommendations submitted by the Kennedy Commission. These recommendations included the repeal of all mandatory minimum statutes and the expanded use of alternatives to incarceration for non-violent offenders.

Mandatory minimum sentences raise serious issues of public policy and routinely result in excessively severe sentences. Mandatory minimum sentences are also frequently arbitrary, because they are based solely on "offense characteristics" and ignore "offender characteristics." They are a large part of the reason why the average length of sentence in the United States has increased threefold since the adoption of mandatory minimums. The United States now imprisons its citizens at a rate roughly five to eight times higher than the countries of Western Europe, and twelve times higher than Japan. Roughly one-quarter of all persons imprisoned in the entire world are imprisoned here in the United States.

Repeal Mandatory Minimums

Thus, the ABA strongly supports the repeal of the existing mandatory minimum penalty for mere possession of crack. Under current law, crack is the only drug that triggers a mandatory minimum for a first offense of simple possession. We would urge the Congress to go farther, however, and repeal mandatory minimum sentences across the board.

We also strongly support the appropriation of funds for developing effective alternatives to incarceration, such as drug courts, intensive supervised treatment programs, and diversionary programs. We know that incarceration does not always rehabilitate—and sometimes has the opposite effect. Drug offenders are peculiarly situated to benefit from such programs, as their crimes are often ones of addiction. That is why last year, after considerable study, research, and public hearings by the ABA's Commission on Effective Sanctions, the ABA's House of Delegates approved a resolution—joined in by the National District Attorneys Association—calling for federal, state, and local governments to develop, support, and fund programs to increase the use of alternatives to incarceration, including for the majority of drug offenders. . . .

In conclusion, for well over a decade the ABA has agreed with the Sentencing Commission's careful analysis that the 100 to 1 quantity ratio is unwarranted and results in penalties that sweep too broadly, apply too frequently to lower-level offenders, overstate the seriousness of the offenses, and produce a large racial disparity in sentencing. Indeed, as the Sentencing Commission noted in its 2007 *Report*, federal cocaine sentencing policy ". . .continues to come under almost universal criticism from representatives of the Judiciary, criminal justice practitioners, academics, and community interest groups . . . [I]naction in this area is of increasing concern to many, including the Commission."

Viewpoint 5

"Prison-bound people who receive [drug] treatment rather than incarceration see lower recidivism . . . rates than those who receive a prison sentence."

Drug Treatment Programs Are a Viable Alternative to Mandatory Minimum Drug Sentences

Justice Policy Institute

The Justice Policy Institute (JPI) is an organization that promotes effective solutions to social problems and is dedicated to ending society's reliance on incarceration as the solution to crime. In the following viewpoint, the organization argues that drug offender alternative sentencing programs have reported significant success in lowering crime and rehabilitating low-level, nonviolent drug offenders.

As you read, consider the following questions:

1. What did Brooklyn's Drug Treatment Alternative-to-Prison Program (DTAP) five-year study show about participants' recidivism rate, according to the author?

Justice Policy Institute, "Effective Investments in Public Safety," 2008. Reproduced by permission.

2. According to a JPI study taken from 2000 to 2005 in Maryland, how did drug rates change in jurisdictions that utilized drug treatment?
3. How did California's Proposition 36 affect the state's violent crime rate between 2000 and 2004, as reported by the author?

A significant number of people arrested and sent to prison are using drugs. While drug use does not predetermine criminality, nearly 29 percent of convicted jail inmates in 2002 reported using drugs at the time of their offense and over 80 percent of all jail inmates reported ever using drugs.

In 2004, about 80 percent of both federal and state prisoners reported ever using drugs, and 53.4 percent of prisoners in state prisons met criteria for drug dependence or abuse. Furthermore, about 25 percent of prisoners incarcerated for violent crimes reported using drugs at the time of their offense.

Whereas in 1980 only about 8% of federal and state prisoners were incarcerated for a drug offense, in 2003, 55 percent of the federal prison population and 20 percent of prisoners in state facilities were incarcerated for drug offenses.

A Maryland Report

In 2002, the Maryland State Commission on Criminal Sentencing Policy reported that 54 percent of cases sentenced on single-count convictions between 1996 and 2001 involved a drug offense. Baltimore's drug imprisonment rate on June 30, 2005 was 453 drug prisoners per 100,000 residents—more than eight times the state median.

In Wisconsin, researchers from Justice Strategies have shown that, "drug prisoners account for more than a fifth of the growth in the sentenced prison population over the last ten years, with close to a third of the growth of prisoners coming from Milwaukee."

Increased Drug Imprisonment Contributes to Prison Expansion

Drug offenses made up almost a third of all state prison sentences in 2002

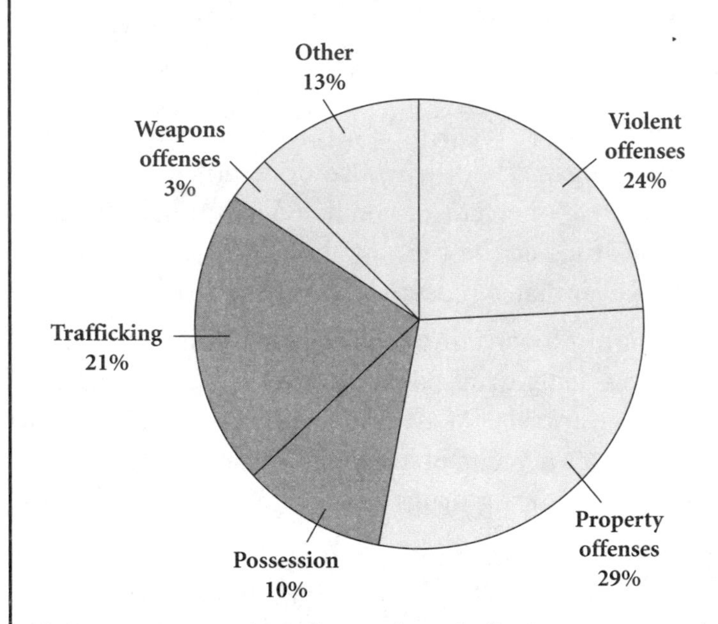

TAKEN FROM: Justice Policy Institute, "Effective Investments in Public Safety: Drug Treatment," 2008; Matthew R. Durose and Patrick A. Langan, 2005. "State Court Sentencing of Convicted Felons, 2002."

Prison-bound people who receive treatment rather than incarceration see lower recidivism [relapse into crime] and re-offending rates than those who receive a prison sentence. A study of adult drug courts in Washington State found that five of the six drug courts reduced recidivism by 13 percent. Furthermore, a review of Washington's Drug Offender Sentencing Alternative (DOSA) program found a 25 percent lower recidivism rate in DOSA participants than in DOSA-eligible non-participants. They found that over a three-year period the re-conviction rate for any felony for DOSA participants was 30.3 percent, compared to 40.5 percent for non-participants. Furthermore, a 2005 study by the WSIPP [Washington State Institute of Public Policy] found that benefits to taxpayers for the DOSA program were between $7 and $10 per dollar spent.

A five-year study of the Drug Treatment Alternative-to-Prison Program (DTAP) in Brooklyn, New York found that DTAP participants had a 26% lower re-arrest rate two years after completing the program than a matched group who went through the standard judicial system. Moreover, the recidivism rate (percentage returning to prison) was 67% lower for DTAP participants than individuals in the comparison group. The study also revealed the cost-effectiveness of the program: the average cost of assigning an individual in DTAP was $32,975 compared to an average cost of $64,338 for incarceration.

DHHS Report

A U.S. Department of Health and Human Services [DHHS] study of thousands of clients receiving drug and alcohol treatment in federally-funded treatment facilities, analyzed the criminal behavior of clients before and after treatment. The study reports that, after treatment, the number of clients selling drugs decreased 78% while the number of people arrested for any crime declined by 64 percent.

The [Maryland] substance abuse treatment department reported the following benefit from drug treatment programs: "Arrest rates during both funded and non-funded treatment were about 75 percent lower than arrest rates during the two years preceding treatment. Arrest rates were reduced by half or more during treatment in most levels of care." In Baltimore City alone, arrests for offenses such as theft, burglary and robbery were 55 percent lower for those who completed treatment than those who did not.

More Treatment Reduces Crime

A Justice Policy Institute study of drug treatment and imprisonment in Maryland from 2000 to 2005 found that eight of

12 jurisdictions that depended more on drug treatment saw crime rates fall by 10 percent or more, while only two of 12 jurisdictions that relied more on imprisonment experienced such a decrease. Of the five counties in Maryland that relied most heavily on drug treatment, all "achieved a major crime-rate reduction" compared to just two of the five counties that depended more heavily on imprisonment.

In California, Proposition 36 was enacted in 2000 to allow individuals convicted of first and second-time drug possession to receive substance abuse treatment instead of incarceration. Despite opponents of Proposition 36, who voiced concerns over rising crime rates if these drug offenders were diverted from prisons, between 2000 and 2004 California's violent crime rate dropped 11.2 percent, over 3 percentage points more than the national crime drop (8.1 percent).

According a Justice Policy Institute study, states with higher levels of drug incarceration have higher levels of drug use. Furthermore, researchers found no basis for the claim that higher drug incarceration rates would deter drug use. This same study found that although New Jersey spends more to incarcerate drug offenders than a third of the states spend on their entire corrections system, it still experiences high levels of drug use.

A Cost-Effective Alternative

A recent study by the Washington State Institute on Public Policy estimated that treatment-oriented programs for those people arrested for drug offenses provided $11,563 in average benefits, per participant. In comparison, drug treatment in prison offered only $7,835 in average benefits per participant.

Between 1988 and 2003, while the national drug control budget grew by 307 percent, marijuana use showed little change. The Office of National Drug Control Policy's fiscal year 2006 budget calls for $7.6 billion in drug law enforcement, while only $3.7 billion is being spent on direct prevention and treatment services.

A 1997 study by the RAND Corporation compared the cost-effectiveness of three programs designed to reduce consumption of cocaine: longer sentences, conventional enforcement and treatment for heavy users. They estimated that treatment is 10 to 15 times more cost-effective by way of reducing drug-related crime than are enforcement interventions.

According to the Final Report of the National Treatment Improvement Evaluation Study (NTIES), published by the Center for Substance Abuse Treatment (CSAT), "treatment appears to be cost effective, particularly when compared to incarceration, which is often the alternative. Treatment costs ranged from a low of $1,800 per client to a high of approximately $6,800 per client."

Periodical Bibliography

The following articles have been selected to supplement the diverse views presented in this chapter.

Erik Eckholm	"Courts Give Addicts a Chance to Straighten Out," *New York Times*, October 14, 2008.
Fred Gardner	"Charles Lynch Gets a Year and a Day (No Thanks to Eric Holder)," *Counterpunch*, June 19, 2009.
Madison Gray	"Mandatory Sentencing: Stalled Reform," *Time*, August 17, 2007.
Angela Hawken and Mark Kleiman	"H.O.P.E. for Reform," *American Prospect*, April 10, 2007.
Jeff Horwitz and Dave Jamieson	"The Two Faces of U.S. Drug Policy," *Atlantic Monthly*, April 8, 2009.
Claudia Kalb	"And Now, Back in the Real World," *Newsweek*, March 3, 2008.
Donna Leinwand	"Study Finds Half of Men Arrested Test Positive for Drugs," *USA Today*, May 28, 2009.
Anthony Papa	"A Slugger's Drug Redemption," *Counterpunch*, July 22, 2008.
Sally Satel	"Medical Misnomer," *Slate*, July 25, 2007.
Kurt L. Schmoke	"Drug Sanity," *New Republic*, April 14, 2008.
Adam Serwer	"Reversing Rockefeller," *American Prospect*, April 1, 2009.
Charles Stimson	"Drug Policy, from Scratch," The Heritage Foundation, April 26, 2008. www.heritage.org.
Washington Post	"Sentences on Trial," October 10, 2008.
Kevin Zeese	"A Break from the Past in the Drug War?" *Counterpunch*, May 8, 2009.

For Further Discussion

Chapter 1

1. Do you think federally mandated minimum jail sentences are effective in the fight to alleviate crime? Why or why not? Consider the evidence and statements given by J. Randy Forbes's and Marc Mauer's testimonies to help formulate and support your answer.
2. Three-strikes laws have proven very controversial. In her viewpoint, Naomi Harlin Goodno argues that despite the problems associated with the law, it has effectively lessened crime in California. Ray Fisman contends, however, that the three-strikes law has resulted in more crime. After reading both viewpoints, where do you stand on the issue? Why?
3. Jodi L. Avergun asserts that mandatory drug sentences work to protect the most vulnerable of citizens and successfully decrease drug and associated crimes. Patrick Leahy counters Avergun by stating that mandatory drug sentences are ineffective in fighting crime. What do you believe are the positive aspects of mandatory drug sentences? What are the problems? Cite from the viewpoints in your answer.

Chapter 2

1. Do you agree with Emily Bazelon that mandatory sentencing is inherently unfair? Or do you concur with Alberto Gonzales, who believes that mandatory sentences are a fair way to deal with criminal behavior? Explain your answer.
2. After reviewing the arguments made by Mike Reynolds and Erwin Chemerinsky, do you think that the three-

strikes law is fair? Would you leave the law as it stands, reform it, or repeal it altogether? Why?

3. In his viewpoint, Chuck Canterbury argues that mandatory crack cocaine possession sentences are an essential weapon for the law enforcement and criminal justice system. He suggests that if anything, the U.S. Sentencing Commission should be considering increasing the mandatory minimum sentences for powder cocaine. Christopher Moraff contends that these crack cocaine possession sentences are unfair, unjust, and ineffective and must be lessened. Which viewpoint do you find more compelling? Why?

Chapter 3

1. Do mandatory drug sentences result in discrimination against blacks? Why or why not? Cite from the viewpoints by Jesselyn McCurdy and Heather Mac Donald to support your argument.
2. Kevin Zeese maintains that mandatory drug sentences waste resources while Judith Greene and Kevin Pranis argue that they result in prison overcrowding. Do you agree with these views? Do you think that the problems associated with mandatory drug sentences are worthwhile? Explain your answers.
3. In his viewpoint, Erik Luna argues that mandatory sentences usurp judicial power by taking away judicial discretion and applying strict mandatory minimum sentences to every case. Do you agree with Luna that judges need the discretion to take into account mitigating circumstances in different cases, or do you think mandatory minimums are beneficial because they provide a standard guideline for all judges to follow? Explain your answer, citing from the viewpoints.

Chapter 4

1. Many experts in the criminal rehabilitation field support the use of drug courts instead of mandatory drug sentences when dealing with drug arrestees, especially for minor offenses. After reading the viewpoints by C. West Huddleston III, Douglas B. Marlowe, and Rachel Casebolt in support of drug courts and Steven K. Erickson's viewpoint in opposition, which view do you think has merit? Why?
2. Of all the viable alternatives, which one mentioned in this chapter do you believe should be used? Explain your answer citing from the viewpoints.

Organizations to Contact

American Civil Liberties Union (ACLU)
125 Broad Street, 18th Floor, New York, NY 10004
(888) 567-ACLU
Web site: www.aclu.org

The American Civil Liberties Union is a national organization that works to protect the rights of individuals and communities as enshrined in the U.S. Constitution. It lobbies Congress to pass legislation protecting civil liberties; employs lawyers to fight discrimination and injustice in court; and organizes activists, volunteers, and other organizations to protest the violation of civil liberties. The ACLU is a strong advocate for the rights of prisoners and is very active in the fight against mandatory minimum sentencing. It publishes in-depth reports of prisoners' rights issues, files briefs on behalf of prisoners, and testifies before Congress and the U.S. Sentencing Commission. The ACLU Web site has a variety of information available on mandatory minimum sentences and prisoners' rights.

Criminal Justice Policy Foundation (CJPF)
8730 Georgia Ave., Suite 400, Silver Spring, MD 20910
(301) 589-6020 • fax: (301) 589-5056
e-mail: info@cjpf.org
Web site: www.cjpf.org

The Criminal Justice Policy Foundation strives to educate the public about the impact of drug policy and the problems of policing on the criminal justice system. It disseminates information and advice to policy-makers, criminal justice professionals, and the public through consultation, education programs, conferences, publications, the news media, and the Internet. Moreover, CJPF assists organizations looking to reform drug sentencing policy with advice on legal organization, management, outreach, research, media relations, and coalition building. The CJPF Web site makes a wide range of research, analyses, and expert testimony available to readers.

Drug Policy Alliance Network (DPA Network)
70 W. Thirty-sixth Street, 16th Floor, New York, NY 10018
(212) 613-8020 • fax: (212) 613-8021
e-mail: nyc@drugpolicy.org
Web site: www.drugpolicy.org

The DPA Network is one of the leading U.S. organizations promoting alternative drug policy. It advocates policies that reduce the harms of both drug misuse and drug prohibition and works to ensure that drug policies no longer arrest, incarcerate, disenfranchise, and otherwise harm millions of nonviolent people. The DPA Network seeks to influence the legislative process by opposing harmful initiatives and promoting sensible drug policy reforms. It has been active in California's Propositions 5 and 36, reforming the Rockefeller Drug Laws in New York, and in the Safety First movement in New Jersey. It has published several in-depth reports on various drugs and their effects on communities, drug policy, and legislative initiatives by experts in the field, which are available on its Web site.

Families Against Mandatory Minimums (FAMM)
1612 K Street NW, Suite 700, Washington, DC 20006
(202) 822-6700 • fax: (202) 822-5704
e-mail: famm@famm.org
Web site: www.famm.org

Families Against Mandatory Minimums promotes comprehensive reforms to mandatory sentencing laws through the legislative process on the federal and state levels, participation in precedent-setting legal cases, and by educating the public on the consequences of mandatory minimum sentencing policies. Its ultimate goal is to reform existing mandatory minimum laws. FAMM members and the public are kept informed on sentencing news through the organization's quarterly newsletter, the *FAMMGram*; its Web site; and monthly e-mails. In fact, FAMM's Web site hosts a wide range of information on congressional hearings and testimony, the latest fact sheets, and recent articles and speeches on the mandatory minimum reform issues. Members can also take action on legislative campaigns through FAMM's Web-based community action network.

Fraternal Order of Police (FOP)

309 Massachusetts Ave. NE, Washington, DC 20002
(202) 547-8189 • fax: (202) 547-8190
e-mail: natlfop@fop.org
Web site: www.fop.net

The largest organization of law enforcement professionals in the United States, the Fraternal Order of Police actively lobbies policy-makers on the issues relevant to rank-and-file law enforcement officers. FOP's National Legislative Program includes matters of sentencing policy, including support of mandatory minimum sentences. The FOP Web site hosts testimony from top officials regarding sentencing policy, changes in the crack-powder disparity, and other criminal justice matters.

Justice Policy Institute (JPI)

1012 Fourteenth Street NW, Suite 400
Washington, DC 20005
(202) 558-7974 • fax: (202) 558-7978
e-mail: info@justicepolicy.org
Web site: www.justicepolicy.org

In 1997 the Justice Policy Institute was founded to advocate for sentencing reform and fair alternatives to incarceration through accessible research, public education, and communications advocacy. JPI strives to alleviate the U.S. reliance on harsh sentencing policy. It promulgates research in a number of related areas, such as juvenile detention, the racial disparity in prison populations, drug policy, and rehabilitation options. JPI has published thorough reports and analyses on the effect of mandatory minimum sentences for drug offenses on Maryland and the failures of the prison industry.

National Association of Drug Court Professionals (NADCP)
4900 Seminary Road, Alexandria, VA 22310
(703) 575-9400
Web site: www.nadcp.org

Founded in 1994, the National Association of Drug Court Professionals is a national nonprofit corporation comprised of judges, prosecutors, defense attorneys, and clinical professionals striving to promote the use of drug courts as an alternative to mandatory minimum sentences for low-level, nonviolent drug offenders. The organization believes that drug courts improve the criminal justice system by using a combination of judicial monitoring and effective treatment to compel drug-using offenders to change their lives. The NADCP advocates the creation of more drug courts, accessible to every community in the United States. For professionals in the field, it offers continuing education and training. It also holds conferences and other events. The NADCP Web site offers a variety of news articles, studies, research papers, and informational pieces on the efficacy of drug courts and the goals of the organization.

The Sentencing Project
514 Tenth Street NW, Suite 1000, Washington, DC 20004
(202) 628-0871 • fax: (202) 628-1091
e-mail: staff@sentencingproject.org
Web site: www.sentencingproject.org

Founded in 1986, the Sentencing Project is a national organization dedicated to changing the way lawmakers, policymakers, and the public think about the U.S. criminal justice system and sentencing policy by promoting reforms in sentencing law and practice and alternatives to incarceration. The Sentencing Project is a leader in the effort to bring national attention to disturbing trends and inequities in the criminal justice system with a successful formula that includes the publication of groundbreaking research, aggressive media campaigns, and strategic advocacy for policy reform. It publishes an annual newsletter and report as well as up-to-date essays, news, fact sheets, and testimony on relevant issues such as sentencing policy, prisoners' rights, women in the criminal justice system, drug policy, and juvenile issues.

Three Strikes and You're Out

PO Box 4163, Fresno, CA 93744
(559) 221-9216 • fax: (559) 221-9288
e-mail: mikereynolds@threestrikes.org
Web site: www.threestrikes.org

The Three Strikes organization was founded by Mike Reynolds, whose daughter was murdered in 1992. This horrific tragedy spurred him to help create and promote California's "three strikes" law, which was implemented in 1994. The Three Strikes Web site provides the most recent information and data on national and California crime rates and prison populations. Reynolds is the author of a book, *Three Strikes and You're Out*, and several essays available on the Web site.

U.S. Sentencing Commission (USSC)

One Columbus Circle NE, Washington, DC 20002-8002
(202) 502-4500
e-mail: pubaffairs@ussc.gov
Web site: www.ussc.gov

Established by the Sentencing Reform Act provisions of the Comprehensive Crime Control Act of 1984, the U.S. Sentencing Commission (USSC) is an independent agency created to (1) to determine sentencing policies and practices for the federal courts, particularly guidelines for the appropriate form and severity of punishment for offenders convicted of federal crimes; (2) to advise and assist Congress and the executive branch in establishing effective and just crime policy; and (3) to collect, analyze, research, and disseminate a variety of information on federal crime and sentencing issues, acting as an information resource for Congress, the executive branch, the courts, criminal justice professionals, and the public. The USSC Web site offers the latest U.S. sentencing guidelines and manuals, up-to-date sentencing statistics, and other relevant publications and resources.

Bibliography of Books

Arthur Benavie	*Drugs: America's Holy War*. New York: Routledge, 2009.
Lawrence V. Brinkley, ed.	*Mandatory Minimum Sentencing: Overview and Background*. Hauppauge, NY: Novinka, 2003.
Alexander Cockburn and Jeffrey St. Clair	*Dime's Worth of Difference: Beyond the Lesser of Two Evils*. Oakland, CA: AK Press, 2004.
Joe Domanick	*Cruel Justice: Three Strikes and the Politics of Crime in America's Golden State*. Berkeley and Los Angeles: University of California Press, 2004.
Joan Esherick	*Prisoner Rehabilitation: Success Stories and Failures*. Philadelphia: Mason Crest, 2007.
Renny Golden	*War on the Family: Mothers in Prison and the Families They Leave Behind*. New York: Routledge, 2005.
Erich Goode	*Drugs in American Society*. San Francisco: McGraw-Hill, 2008.
Kelly Hannah-Moffat and Pat O'Malley, eds.	*Gendered Risks*. New York: Routledge-Cavendish, 2007.
Craig Hemmens, ed.	*Current Legal Issues in Criminal Justice*. New York: Oxford University Press, 2007.

David L. Hudson — *Race, Ethnicity, and the American Criminal Justice System*. Chicago: American Bar Association, 2005.

Laura E. Huggins — *Drug War Deadlock: The Policy Battle Continues*. Stanford, CA: Hoover Institution Press, 2005.

Michael Jacobson — *Downsizing Prisons: How to Reduce Crime and Mass Incarceration*. New York: New York University Press, 2005.

Douglas W. Kieso — *Unjust Sentencing and the California Three Strikes Law*. New York: LFB, 2005.

John Kroger — *Convictions: A Prosecutor's Battles Against Mafia Killers, Drug Kingpins, and Enron Thieves*. New York: Farrar, Straus, and Giroux, 2008.

James E. Lessenger and Glade F. Roper, eds. — *Drug Courts: A New Approach to Treatment and Rehabilitation*. New York: Springer, 2007.

Mitchell B. Mackinem and Paul Higgins — *Drug Court: Construct the Moral Identity of Drug Offenders*. Springfield, IL: C.C. Thomas, 2008.

Marc Mauer — *Race to Incarcerate*. New York: New Press, 2006.

Doris Marie Provine — *Unequal Under the Law: Race in the War on Drugs*. Chicago: University of Chicago Press, 2007.

Nancy Rodriguez *Persistent Offender Law: Racial Disparity, Patterned Offenses, and Unintended Effects*. New York: LFB, 2003.

Thomas C. Rowe *Federal Narcotics Laws and the War on Drugs: Money Down a Rat Hole*. Binghamton, NY: Haworth, 2006.

Courtney Semisch *Alternative Sentencing in the Federal Criminal Justice System*. Washington, DC: United States Sentencing Commission, 2009.

Merrill Singer *Drugging the Poor: Legal and Illegal Drugs and Social Inequality*. Long Grove, IL: Waveland Press, 2008.

Jennifer E. Walsh *Three Strikes Law*. Westport, CT: Greenwood, 2007.

David B. Wolcott *Crime and Punishment in America*. New York: Facts On File, 2008.

Index

H

I

J

N

O

S

T

W

Y

Z